THE EVANGELIST OF DESIRE

Josiah Wedgwood, "Portrait Medallion of John Wesley," c. 1785 (formerly in the possession of the Davison Art Center Collection, Wesleyan University, Middletown, Connecticut).

The Evangelist of Desire

JOHN WESLEY

AND THE

METHODISTS

Henry Abelove

Stanford University Press, Stanford, California

1990

Stanford University Press
Stanford, California
© 1990 by the Board of Trustees of the
Leland Stanford Junior University
Printed in the United States of America

CIP data appear at the end of the book

To my mother and
the memory of my father

Acknowledgments

Many people have helped me to write this book. Some have taught me history or theory, some have done chores for me, some have encouraged me. As a sign of my lasting gratitude to them, I list their names here: Sydney Ahlstrom, Nancy Armstrong, Charles Brenner, Daniel Cantor, Anthony Carlo, Samuel Cohn, Ellen D'Oench, Kate Gilbert, David Halperin, Neil Hertz, Patricia Hill, Gail Malmgreen, William Ian Miller, Richard Ohmann, Martin Price, Jordan Rau, Joseph W. Reed, Jr., Phyllis Rose, Donna Scott, Eve Kosofsky Sedgwick, Bernard Semmel, Ann-Louise Shapiro, Gary Spear, Leonard Tennenhouse, Randolph Trumbach, Richard T. Vann, Clarence Walker, John Walsh, Jeffrey Weeks, and Stephen D. White.

I am obliged to the Methodist Archive at the John Rylands University Library of Manchester for permitting me to quote extensively from their manuscript collection; to the Beinecke Rare Book and Manuscript Library at Yale University for permitting me to quote from William E. Park's manuscript biography of Jonathan Edwards; to Farrar, Straus, and Giroux, Inc., for permitting me to quote from Robert Lowell, *For the Union Dead* © 1960, 1964; to the Reverend Dr. Frank Baker for permitting me to quote from the manuscript diary of Thomas Illingworth; to the Pierpont Morgan Library for providing me with a photograph of the 1757 manuscript class list of the Kingswood Methodist Society; to the Davison Art Center at Wesleyan University, the Olin Library at Wesleyan University, and the National Gallery of Canada, Ottawa, for permitting me to reproduce photographs of art works in their collections.

Acknowledgments are due to Wesleyan University and to Routledge and Kegan Paul for permitting me to reprint revised versions of articles of mine. "The Basis of Wesley's Influence: Deference" was published originally in *Wesleyan Library Notes* (No. 16, 1982), and "The Sexual Politics of Early Wesleyan Methodism" was published originally in *Disciplines of Faith*, ed. by Jim Obelkevich, Lyndal Roper, and Raphael Samuel (London and New York, 1987).

H.A.

Contents

Four pages of illustrations follow p. 38

Preface

. . . for I
Except you enthrall me, never shall be free,
Nor ever chast, except you ravish mee.
—John Donne

Early English Methodism is a much-studied subject. But when I started to work on it, I had an angle of approach all my own. I wanted to ask: how did John Wesley succeed in attracting to himself so many long-staying followers? Of what he taught these followers once he had attracted them, how much did they really accept?

Hardly anyone had focused on just these questions before. Most writers on Methodism had been content with perfunctory explanations of Wesley's success in attracting a following. They had usually said either that he was a good organizer or that he preached a plain and understandable Christian message which was naturally appealing. Most had been similarly quick in judging the extent of his influence. They had usually assumed that what Wesley taught, his followers had learned.

I could tell that these old views were weak. I knew that Wesley had never been an especially good organizer, that virtually all the organizational initiatives in early Methodism had come from his followers and sometimes over his strong objections. I knew too that Wesley's message, however plain and Christian, had hardly been exceptional; that he had preached in an era of wide revival; and that scores of evangelists had said doctrinally much the same as he and at much the same time but without comparable success in attracting a following. I knew, furthermore, that Wesley's followers had rejected or modified at least some of his teachings in practice. There was readily available evidence to show, for instance, that neither his notion of perfection (Wesley thought that any converted Christian could become morally perfect before death) nor his ban on smuggling had been truly accepted.

In beginning research, I felt I had an interesting and demanding inquiry ahead of me. I do not recall that I had any expectation that the inquiry would force me to think much about sex.

Yet as I worked, I learned that religion and sex, at least in the case of early Methodism, were intermixed. If Wesley was successful in attracting to himself a long-staying following, that was largely because he was both seductive and monopolistic. I found, for instance, that he made his followers fall in love with him, and that he tried to prevent them from marrying. I learned also that the Methodists never simply accepted what he taught and demanded; that though they loved him as he wanted them to, they felt united to one another as well; that in that union they discovered common needs; and that they resisted him and modified what he demanded until they managed to transform it into something that suited them.

In the book that follows, I report fully on what I found. The book is not a biography of Wesley, though I do include some new information about him. I give a fairly close account of a few episodes in his life, but only because they disclose so much about his interaction with his followers. Nor is the book a socioeconomic profile of the early Methodist community. Such a profile, based on detailed local studies, would be useful, but I do not provide it. What I do in this book is describe and analyze a relationship between one man, a gentleman and a preacher, and the thousands of plebeians, women, men, and children, whom he took to himself and tried to lead. My theme is seduction, resistance, and the cultural consequences of both.

THE EVANGELIST OF DESIRE

Chapter One

The Problem Stated

Anyone who hears the word Methodism is likely to think first of John Wesley, the original leader of the movement. For his life has long since been made into story, and the story is almost as familiar as a legend.

Born at Epworth, in the marsh country of Lincolnshire, where his father was the parish clergyman and his mother was a pious co-laborer, Wesley grew up with many brothers and sisters in a big, thatched rectory. When he was just five years old, the rectory caught fire, and he was rescued at the last moment. His mother called him ever after "the brand plucked from the burning" and encouraged him to believe that God had saved him from the fire so that he might eventually do some special work. As a young man he went up to Oxford, where in the course of time he took orders, won election to a fellowship, and joined a private, religious club.

In this club, whose members included one of his brothers, Charles, and a young man named George Whitefield, Wesley assumed a leading role. Under his guidance the members kept a strict regimen. They fasted, took communion frequently, observed the Sabbath, met together for prayer and study, and visited the prisoners in the local jail, whom they fed and taught and comforted. So regular, so methodical, was their piety that the wits of the university jokingly called them "Methodists." Despite the jokes, the club flourished, but Wesley grew to feel that Oxford was somehow the wrong place for him, and when an opportunity offered to serve as a clergyman in the newly opening colony of Georgia, he accepted eagerly. He spent about two years in Georgia and then returned to England.

While abroad he had met some German pietists whose lives had struck him as more rightly Christian than his own. In England again, 'he fell in with others like them and learned from their teaching that he had been wrong to make his religion consist chiefly of a regimen of good works. They said that he should recognize his sinfulness, repent, and believe that God would both forgive him and provide him with an instantaneous assurance of forgiveness. Wesley tried hard to do as they said, and one evening while attending the meeting of a club in London like the one he had formerly led at Oxford, he felt his heart, as he later wrote in his Journal, "strangely warmed"; and he knew at once that he had been saved.

This experience of forgiveness, this conversion, opened a new epoch in his career. Although he still held his Oxford fellowship, he refrained from settling back into university life; instead, he went to work preaching wherever he could borrow a pulpit, and also out-of-doors, and traveled throughout the kingdom in an ever-widening arc. He coordinated his efforts with his brother Charles and with Whitefield, who had both undergone conversion, too, and who were preaching and traveling as he was.

Nearly everywhere he preached, some of his hearers experienced convictions of their sinfulness, often also full conversions like his own, and they clustered to him for further guidance. Most of them were plebeians. He brought them together into what he called societies, local membership chapters. At their urging, he also started leasing and building rooms for their meetings. These he called preaching-houses. Again at their urging, he started appointing laymen to preach to them. These lay preachers he called helpers. Yet again at their urging, he divided each society into smaller groups that were to meet weekly for dues-paying and for mutual edification and support. These smaller groups he called classes. Soon the name that had stuck to the Oxford club revived, and his followers came to be known as Methodists.

As the years passed his energy never slackened. He kept preaching, traveling, and taking pastoral charge of those of his hearers who clustered to him. He gave them rules of conduct; published books, pamphlets, and journals for them; and presided over their societies, preaching-houses, classes, and a growing band of helpers. Some of his fellow Church of England clergymen disapproved of his work and charged him with promoting "enthusiasm," but this charge he bore with equanimity and continued on his way. All in all he traveled some 250,000 miles and preached some 40,000 sermons. When he died in 1791, his followers, the Methodists, by then a vast, far-flung, and highly organized body, mourned him as a "prince and great man fallen this day in Israel."

That is the well-known story, and almost equally well known is the judgment of the historians, that Wesley's conversion and the pastoral labors devolving from it were enormously influential, "meant more for Britain," as one nineteenth-century observer said, "than all the victories of Pitt by land and sea."[1] So far the unanimity of opinion goes but no further. For Wesley's influence, acknowledged on every side as enormous, is differently assessed and evaluated. Some say that his impact on English plebeians was repressive.[2] Others say that it was progressive, modernizing, revolutionary.[3]

One problem about these varying evaluations of his influence may be that they are all oddly premature. Nobody has ever determined what exactly his influence was. It cannot be assumed, or rather it can be assumed only naïvely, that what Wesley taught was what the Methodists learned. To discover how they reacted to him, what they actually absorbed of what he taught, must be a matter for actual inquiry. Two questions in particular need to be asked and answered. First, just how did Wesley get to be as influential on so many English plebeians as he undoubtedly was? Second, how did they respond to what he told them? These are the questions that will be considered here.

Before the first of these two questions is broached, some preliminary observations are in order. At the time that Wesley began his ex-

---

[1] William Hartpole Lecky, *A History of England in the Eighteenth Century* (London, 1883), 2:521.

[2] This was of course the view of Élie Halévy. For his thinking on this matter, see Bernard Semmel's introduction to his translation of Élie Halévy, *The Birth of Methodism in England* (Chicago, 1971), pp. 1–29. It is also the view of E. P. Thompson, though his position is distinguishable from Halévy's: Halévy contended that Methodism prevented anything like the French Revolution from happening in England, whereas Thompson thought that Methodism was intrinsically a part of the counterrevolution. See E. P. Thompson, *The Making of the English Working Class* (rev. ed.; London, 1968), especially p. 419.

[3] Bernard Semmel, *The Methodist Revolution* (New York, 1973), especially pp. 8–22.

traordinary pastorate to the British people, in the late 1730's, virtually the whole Protestant world was undergoing an evangelical awakening.[4] In England many preachers besides him and his clerical collaborators and his band of helpers were crisscrossing the countryside, giving sermons and exhortations, and evoking a strong response from their hearers. Some of these preachers are noticed in the pages of the Journal that Wesley himself published: Howel Harris, the Welshman; David Culey, whose followers were called the Culeymites; the group of preachers patronized by the Countess of Huntingdon; Benjamin Ingham, who like Wesley brought his followers together in societies; the six women who itinerated around the town of Wells, all of them members of the Church of England.[5] Others, although unnoticed in Wesley's Journal, were also active: for instance, Philip Doddridge, the prominent Dissenter, who made preaching tours from his base at Northampton, or the "itinerant mendicant" clergyman of the Church of England, whose name was Holt, and who turned up one night at a house in Preston and slept there before continuing to wander.[6]

Outside England too the waves of the revival ran strong. In Scotland hundreds, maybe thousands, were converted in the neighborhoods of Cambuslang and Kilsyth and throughout the Highlands.[7] In Germany pietists like the ones that Wesley met while he was abroad were preaching, traveling, and, at Herrnhut, founding a com-

---

[4]And maybe more than just the Protestant world. It is possible that the Jewish and the Catholic worlds were both affected by the same great movement. The beginning of Jewish Hasidism is exactly contemporary, and the convulsionaries of St. Medard, roughly so.

[5]Nehemiah Curnock, ed., *The Journal of the Rev. John Wesley, A.M.* (London, 1909–16), 2: 223; 3: 61; 2: 483; 6: 241, 338.

[6]William Dobson, ed., *Extracts from the Diary of the Rev. Peter Walkden, Non-Conformist Minister, for the Years 1725, 1729, and 1730* (Preston, 1866), p. 112. Doddridge's preaching tours are noted by Alan Everitt, *The Pattern of Rural Dissent* (Leicester, 1972), p. 52. Wesley did refer to Doddridge but not as a fellow itinerant.

[7]For the revivals at Cambuslang and Kilsyth and their environs, see the summary ministerial reports in John Gillies, ed., *Historical Collections Relating to the Remarkable Success of the Gospel, and Eminent Instruments Employed in Promoting It* (Glasgow, 1754), 2: 339–402. On the revival in the Highlands, see John Macinnes, *The Evangelical Movement in the Highlands of Scotland, 1688–1800* (Aberdeen, 1951). On Scottish piety generally, see Marilyn J. Westerkamp, *Triumph of the Laity* (New York, 1988).

munity.[8] In the North American colonies in 1740, revivalist preachers, aided by Wesley's collaborator Whitefield, who was on tour there, elicited a terrific, unprecedented response from their hearers. For some years after, much of the countryside was awash with revivalist fervor. This revival is remembered as the Great Awakening.[9]

One feature of Wesley's revival, of Methodism, distinguishes it from the others. It lasted, getting bigger and bigger all the while, at least as long as Wesley lived. When he died in 1791, the Methodists owned 588 preaching-houses in the British Isles, and their members numbered 72,476.[10] The other revivals that had begun at about the same time as Wesley's turned out differently. In the North American colonies the revivalist wave ebbed almost immediately after it had crested. It was mostly gone by 1749, fully gone by 1760.[11] In Germany the pietists at Herrnhut maintained their community, but just maintained it, and came to be more and more isolated and idiosyncratic with the passing of time; certainly they showed no capacity there for dynamic expansion.[12] In Scotland the revivalist wave ebbed as completely and almost as fast as it had in the colonies.[13] As for the Countess of Huntingdon's Connection, that proved evanescent too. She

[8]For a sociological study of the Moravian strain in German evangelicalism, see Gillian Gollin, *Moravians in Two Worlds* (New York, 1967).

[9]There are many studies on the Great Awakening in the North American colonies. See, for instance, the old but still useful bibliography in Richard Bushman, ed., *The Great Awakening* (Williamsburg, Va., 1970). For a recent overview, see David S. Lovejoy, *Religious Enthusiasm in the New World* (Cambridge, Mass., 1985), pp. 178–214. Christine Heyrman, *Commerce and Culture* (New York, 1984), provides a recent local study of revivalism in Gloucester and Marblehead.

[10]Frank Baker, "The People Called Methodists: 3. Polity," in Rupert Davies and Gordon Rupp, *A History of the Methodist Church in Great Britain* (London, 1965), 1: 228; John Walsh, "Methodism at the End of the Eighteenth Century," in ibid., p. 278.

[11]In New England it was gone even earlier, by 1742 or 1744. Edwin W. Gaustad, *The Great Awakening in New England* (New York, 1957), pp. 61–79. It is possible to represent the Great Awakening as lasting beyond 1760, but only by arguing that the Revolution was somehow both a continuation and a fulfillment of the awakening. For an instance of such an argument, see William G. McLoughlin, *Revivals, Awakenings, and Reform* (Chicago, 1978), p. 97. For a strong critique of such arguments, see Jon Butler, "Enthusiasm Described and Decried," *Journal of American History*, 69 (1982): 305–25.

[12]Gollin, pp. 214–15.

[13]Gillies, 2: 393, 397.

died the same year as Wesley, and by then her flock owned only seven chapels. Between fifty-five and eighty other chapels were loosely associated with her Connection, but they mostly went independent or disappeared entirely during the years immediately following.[14] This distinction between Methodism and the other contemporary revivals—that it lasted and steadily grew while they did not—should be remembered as the first of our two basic questions is considered: how did Wesley manage to influence plebeians so successfully?

[14]Walsh, "Methodism at the End of the Eighteenth Century," p. 292.

Chapter Two

The Basis of
Wesley's Influence:
Deference

Wesley influenced English plebeians first by the most usual means of all. He played the gentleman, and he exacted deference.

As he traveled from place to place, he made his status clear by his clothes and grooming. Ordinarily he appeared in a gown, cassock, and bands,[1] the canonically correct dress of a clergyman of the Church of England, and a sign of gentility, of course, as much as of profession. He wore also silk stockings and gloves and, when the weather was cold, a floor-length brocaded cloak.[2] At his breast he had a gold stickpin, and on his shoes, as a Yarm woman noticed, "large silver buckles."[3] He kept himself neat and fastidiously clean, and he took pains with his hair. It was his own, not a wig,[4] and he wore it long, parted in the middle, combed straight back, and curling slightly at the bottom. To some of his fellow gentlemen the hair seemed almost too arranged, too pretty. An undergraduate who saw him on the

[1] Nehemiah Curnock, ed., *The Journal of the Rev. John Wesley, A.M.* (London, 1909–16), 3: 95; 5: 176; 6: 303.

[2] Luke Tyerman, *The Life and Times of the Rev. John Wesley, A.M.* (2d ed.; London, 1870–72), 2: 409; Curnock, 7: 416; Frederick Gill, *In the Steps of John Wesley* (London, 1962), pp. 72–73. For a general account of the dress of the well-to-do, see Anne Buck, *Dress in Eighteenth-Century England* (New York, 1979), pp. 25–102.

[3] *The Homes, Haunts, and Friends of John Wesley; Being the Centenary Number of the Methodist Recorder* (rev. and enlarged ed.; London, 1891), p. 135; Yarm woman quoted by Tyerman, *Life and Times*, 2: 409.

[4] Wesley was ill in June 1775, and as a result of the illness, lost his hair. He did wear a wig for some months after, but only until the hair grew back. See G. Stringer Rowe, "John Wesley's Wig," *Proceedings of the Wesley Historical Society*, 6 (June 1907): 27–28.

last occasion he preached at Oxford commented, for instance, on how "very exactly" it was parted; and Horace Walpole, who saw him once at Bath, and observed the hair particularly, told a correspondent, with some malice, about "the little soupçon of curl at the ends."[5] But to a Buxton man Wesley looked perfect, like somebody from another world, "like an angel," and his hair, just "beautiful."[6]

Wesley made his status clear also by his style of living and traveling. From 1739 until his death in 1791, he kept lodgings in London—first, a suite of rooms, then later a three-story town house.[7] He stayed at these lodgings, and centered his work in London, for about four months every year. A staff of servants waited on him and on any of the helpers who might be there.[8] Whenever he left London to go on a country preaching tour, he traveled genteelly. During the early part of his career, he usually rode on horseback; after 1766, he usually traveled in his own carriage, a big chaise custom-fitted with a bookcase inside.[9] Whether on horseback or in the carriage, he never went alone. He took at least one companion with him[10]—and often more. On one of his tours his retinue of servants, helpers, and sympathizers was so numerous that when he came to cross the Irish Sea, he could accommodate them only by hiring a whole packet-boat.[11]

Then, too, wherever Wesley traveled he offered to perform a conventionally genteel function, to doctor people without charge. When the poor were sick they could seldom afford to go to a physician or an apothecary.[12] Instead they might go for doctoring to the back door of a nearby rectory or great house where, applying as dependents,

---

[5]Elijah Hoole, "Dr. Kennicott and Mr. Wesley's Last Sermon at St. Mary's, Oxford," *Wesleyan Methodist Magazine*, 5th series, 12 (Jan. 1866): 47; Curnock, 5: 189.

[6]Curnock, 6: 413.

[7]John Telford, *Wesley's Chapel and Wesley's House* (rev. ed.; London, 1926), p. 19.

[8]Curnock, 6: 49.

[9]Tyerman, *Life and Times*, 2: 409. This carriage was a bequest from an admirer. See John Telford, ed., *The Letters of the Rev. John Wesley, A.M.* (London, 1931), 5: 20.

[10]John Whitehead, *The Life of the Rev. John Wesley, A.M., Sometime Fellow of Lincoln College, Oxford, Collected from His Private Papers and Printed Works. . . .* (London, 1796), 2: 370.

[11]Curnock, 7: 299.

[12]An apothecary might charge from one to three shillings for a dose of medicine, a physician usually a guinea for a consultation. See Lester King, *The Medical World of the Eighteenth Century* (Chicago, 1958), p. 10.

they might get broth or wine or common drugs or advice as a favor. They could similarly apply to Wesley. At Leigh he dispensed free pills to a woman and her two children, all stricken with the ague, who presented themselves at the door of the house where he was dining; at Ballybofey he treated a "poor man" who was vomiting blood; at Lisburn he devoted all his spare time to seeing a sequence of "poor patients."[13]

Finally, Wesley grew rich publishing tracts, sermons, journals, and pamphlets, and he gave away much money. At his death one newspaper, *The London Chronicle*, said that he had lately been making £10,000 a year.[14] This figure was meant to sound sensational and was almost certainly exaggerated. One of his followers, who was a bookseller and therefore in a favorable position to know, suggested a likelier figure—£2,000 a year.[15] But even if Wesley's income at the height of his career was only half that, only £1,000 a year, it was still at a rough comparison as big as, or bigger than, the revenues of eight of the bishoprics of the Church of England.[16] That income he deployed in genteel and open-handed charity, not only providing coal, bread, and clothes for the needy, especially the needy among his followers, whom he visited house-to-house and oversaw closely, but also creating make-work for the unemployed and, on one occasion, assuming responsibility for an orphaned child.[17]

[13]Curnock, 4: 188; 5: 127, 513. See also George S. Rousseau, "John Wesley's Primitive Physick, 1747," *Harvard Library Bulletin*, 16 (1968): 242–56. For a general account of the importance of the benefactions of well-to-do laypeople in eighteenth-century English medicine, see Roy Porter, "Medicine and the Enlightenment in Eighteenth-Century England," *Society for the Social History of Medicine Bulletin*, 25 (1979): 33, 38.

[14]Quoted in *Homes, Haunts, and Friends*, p. 150.

[15]*Memoirs of James Lackington, Written by Himself* (New York, 1796), p. 26.

[16]Nehemiah Curnock, the Methodist antiquary who prepared the edition of Wesley's Journal currently used by scholars, said that the income may have been £1,000 in some years. This was a very cautious estimate. See *Homes, Haunts, and Friends*, p. 150. And if Wesley's income was double that amount, £2,000 a year, it was at a rough comparison as big as, or bigger than, the revenues of *eighteen* of the bishoprics of the Church of England. I base these comparisons on the estimates of the revenues of the bishoprics for the year 1762 provided by D. Hirschberg, "A Social History of the Anglican Episcopate, 1660–1760" (Ph.D. dissertation, University of Michigan, 1976), pp. 373–76.

[17]Curnock, 3: 332.

Sometimes, however, despite gown, cassock, bands, silk, gold, silver, hair, servants, London house, country touring, retinue, horses, carriage, doctoring, riches, charity—despite all the appurtenances of gentility—Wesley did not immediately get the deference he wanted. He got resistance instead. "Unbroken spirits,"[18] as he called the people of Manchester, would surround him and jeer him and perhaps threaten him with violence. At such times he would need courage, and it never failed him. What he did in Manchester, when a big, threatening crowd followed after him one day as he strode toward a central spot to preach, was to turn on them "abruptly," face them, and try to talk them into recognizing what he was, what his position was, and what he felt was his due. He told them that he had once preached and administered the sacrament in a "neighboring church," that many of them had "seen" him there. This quelled them, at least for the moment, and he could start to preach.[19] Similarly at Redmire, when he rode into town and found the people staring hostilely, as if he and his retinue were "a company of monsters," he stepped into the street and announced that the older people in the crowd had "seen" him preach at Wensley Church thirty years before. Again the hostility subsided and he was able to give his sermon; and as he rode out of town two hours later, he had the satisfaction of noting that the people were altogether changed, that they were "bowing and curt-seying on every side."[20]

In some places Wesley could make little progress, no matter how firmly he insisted on his due. For the "unbroken spirits" were backed by a local squire or parson, who strongly resented the intrusion into his own domain of a strange new master. This backing might take any of several forms. As Wesley would try to preach to a boisterous, perhaps an angry crowd, the local opposer, squire or parson, might stand by and lead the jeering, or encourage it by tossing the crowd money, or supplement it by hiring somebody to ring the church bells nonstop.[21] Perhaps more commonly the local opposer might stay at home. He might content himself with talking against Wesley before his arrival, calling him a subversive Roundhead or a subversive Jaco-

---

[18] Ibid., p. 295.
[19] Ibid.
[20] Ibid., 6: 26.
[21] For example, ibid., 3: 368–89; 4: 136, 331.

bite, and hinting that anything the crowd might care to do in welcoming him, short of mayhem, would be winked at by the gentlemen of the neighborhood.[22] Possibly the local opposer might take a more moderate line. He might, as magistrate, protect Wesley from annoyance but make his own views clear nonetheless. One squire, Sir Francis Vyvyan, let his people know that anybody who went to hear Wesley preach would never again be admitted to the annual Christmas feast at the Vyvyan great house.[23]

During the course of Wesley's fifty-one years as a traveling evangelist, some of his local opposers were removed out of his way, as he thought, providentially. One "dropped down and spoke no more"; another hanged himself in "his own necessary house"; two in the same parish were "snatched away by a fever."[24] It is also true that as the years passed, and as Wesley came to be a more familiar figure in the countryside, his local opposers grew quieter. He even found a few squires and parsons, though just a few, who favored him and supported his efforts to influence their people. At Monmouth a squire offered to put him up overnight, and in consequence "all the rabble in town were quiet as lambs." At Passage a gentleman joined the crowd around Wesley and kept them in order. Otherwise, as Wesley later noted in his Journal, they would surely have been "rude." But they "stood in awe" of the gentleman, whose name was Freestone, and

who gave one and another, when they did not regard his signs, a stroke on the head with his stick. By this means the whole multitude was tolerably quiet, and many seemed much affected.[25]

Most local powers, however, were neither removed out of his way nor inclined to give him the sort of welcome help he got at Monmouth and Passage. Most threw their weight into the scale against him. So general and so firm was their opposition that wherever they were, Wesley had little success in gaining followers. He made headway mostly in those places where there was no strong squire or parson to resent his intrusion—in the out-townships of geographically big

[22]For example, ibid., 4: 468.
[23]Ibid., 3: 192.
[24]Ibid., 3: 387; 4: 133, 529.
[25]Ibid., 6: 316; 5: 320.

parishes, in new, fast-growing industrial settlements, in parishes with nonresident or pluralist clergymen,[26] and in populous cities like London, Bristol, Newcastle, and Dublin. Here, where no dominating local power could hinder him, Wesley made his greatest impact; here he built Methodism; here he gathered his sheep.

Wesley contended, then, with powerful local opposers for the prize of the deference of the people. He also contended for the same prize with his colleagues, his fellow evangelists.

Wesley respected and valued these fellow evangelists—the helpers, his brother Charles, George Whitefield. He believed that all were engaged in the work of God. Still, he considered them rivals, and he tried to undercut them. Whitefield had come from a poor family, had worked for a while as a tap-boy in an inn at Gloucester, and had entered the university as a "servitor." As an adult he retained an accent and some mannerisms that were ungenteel. Wesley's way of jabbing at him, of depreciating his status, was to compliment him backhandedly on his success as a preacher. In the Journal that Wesley periodically published, he wrote of how helpful Whitefield was to those poor people who found the "little improprieties both of his language and manner" congenial.[27] Even Charles got hit. Wesley jabbed at him covertly, complaining without naming—writing, for instance, that Charles had been preaching in Ireland and then remarking, immediately after, that somebody there had sent exaggerated accounts of the growth of the movement, or writing that Charles had been preaching in Newcastle and then remarking, immediately after, that the people there knew nothing of early morning prayers.[28]

Wesley wrote carefully about these men, so nearly his peers; he kept his criticism muted, his depreciation of their status indirect. But in writing in the Journal about his helpers, the mostly low-born laymen whom he employed to preach in his wake, he was openly scornful. "Raw young men," he called them, "without name, learning, or eminent sense."[29] Sometimes he carried the depreciation beyond

---

[26]Robert Currie, "A Micro-Theory of Methodist Growth," *Proceedings of the Wesley Historical Society*, 36 (Oct. 1967): 65–73.

[27]Curnock, 3: 452. For a comment in the same style about the evangelist Howel Harris, see ibid., 2: 296.

[28]Ibid., 3: 50, 338.

[29]Ibid., 4: 54. This description, too, was part of a backhanded compliment.

words into action. He would require a helper accompanying him on a preaching tour to double as a servant, as a groom maybe or as a valet.[30] Even when he took no measure so strong as that, he kept the helpers subordinate. He always retained the right to hire and fire them, and he supervised their conduct, too. In fact he promulgated twelve rules, meant to guide them in everything. These rules specified, for instance, how they were to spend their time ("never be triflingly employed"), how they were to talk with women ("sparingly and cautiously"), and how they were to deport themselves ("be serious"). Wesley wanted especially to keep the helpers from presuming socially. So the rules included also a firm prohibition: "Do nothing as a gentleman. You have no more to do with this character than with that of a dancing master."[31]

In their subordinate role the helpers found that the preaching work they wanted to do was poignantly hard. They had been called to their vocation by Wesley, and naturally he was their model. But they were restrained partly by their own social background, still more by his supervision, his firm rule, from being entirely like him. They were restrained from exacting deference on their own.

He, as an ordained clergyman, might wear gown, cassock, bands; they were unordained, and he urged them to stay unordained.[32] They could under no circumstances dress canonically as clergymen. He might wear gold, silver, silk, brocade; for them such splendor was of course disallowed. It would have been genteel. One helper tried to dress up quietly, unsplendidly. He wore a "slouch hat," a style then fashionable. But Wesley caught sight of the hat and got angry, said that it was an insult to him personally. So the slouch hat had to be instantly sacrificed.[33]

[30] Telford, *Letters*, 3: 140.

[31] *Minutes of the Methodist Conferences* (London, 1862), 1: 24. For an account of the successive editions of the twelve rules and their textual variation, see "The Twelve Rules of a Helper," *Proceedings of the Wesley Historical Society*, 7 (Dec. 1909): 82–83.

[32] When Wesley was 81 years old and wanted to establish a succession, he changed his mind about the desirability of ordination for the helpers. I discuss his change of mind in Chap. 8.

[33] James Everett, *Adam Clarke Portrayed* (London, 1843), 2: 12. For an account of the new availability of fashionable consumer items like slouch hats, see Neil

A few of the helpers tried a different tack. Instead of dressing up, at the risk of provoking Wesley's anger, they ventured to assert themselves in another way. They attempted to display, by various means, the kinds of work they had once done. One helper, who had been by trade a tailor, kept a pincushion fashioned onto his right elbow as he preached.[34] Another, once a stonemason, preached with a hammer and trowel tucked under his overall.[35] A third, who had served in the army and liked to be called "Captain," preached in full regimentals with a sword laid across the pages of the Bible opened in front of him.[36] Most of the helpers, however, took gradually to dressing alike, probably out of solidarity, and the costume they evolved was a plain blue suit.[37] It was easy to acquire, was humble enough to be acceptable to Wesley, and communicated just a smothered hint of status. For blue was the color favored by Church of England clergymen, at least for leisure wear.[38]

Hair was a problem too. If the helpers wore their own, they might find that the public disapproved. Natural hair was unusual; it was a style very hard to make attractive, and anyway it had been virtually preempted by Wesley. One helper, whose hair was short and curly, very unlike Wesley's, wore it naturally and drew a hostile reaction

---

McKendrick, "The Commercialization of Fashion," in Neil McKendrick, John Brewer, and J. H. Plumb, eds., *The Birth of a Consumer Society* (London, 1983), pp. 34–99.

[34] Richard Treffrey, *Memoirs of Mr. Richard Trewavas, Sr., of Mousehole, Cornwall* (London, 1839), pp. 37–44.

[35] Curnock, 3: 12.

[36] Charles Atmore, *The Methodist Memorial; Being An Impartial Sketch of the Lives and Characters of the Preachers, Who Have Departed This Life Since the Commencement of the Work of God Among the People Called Methodists . . . Rev. John Wesley, Deceased* (Bristol, 1801), p. 446; Frank Baker, *Charles Wesley as Revealed by His Letters* (London, 1948), p. 88. This helper was "Captain" Thomas Webb. He had never really held a captaincy. W. A. Goss, "Early Methodism in Bristol," *Proceedings of the Wesley Historical Society*, 19 (Sept. 1934): 166.

[37] S. L. Coupe, James Howarth, and Hugh Taylor, *Wesleyan Methodism in Bagslate* (Bagslate, 1910), p. 5.

[38] Note the reaction that the helper Thomas Olivers drew from the local squire. "When my Lord saw me, he said, 'Wh-wh-why, dost thou dress like a Parson?' (For I was dressed in blue)." Thomas Jackson, ed., *The Lives of Early Methodist Preachers, Chiefly written by Themselves* (London, 1838), 1: 216. See also, for the term "parson's blue," "The Connoisseur," no. 65 (1823), 25: 367.

from a Bristol man, who had come to hear the preaching. "A thick head of curled hair," the Bristol man said, disgusted, "resembling a mop."[39] Another helper (a clerical sympathizer, really), whose hair was rather like Wesley's, wore it naturally and got charged with seeming "to ape Mr. John in the mode of wearing his hair."[40] On the other hand the helpers could hardly wear wigs if they were fancy— equipped, say, with bags or tied-back queues. That sort of headgear was an option disallowed as certainly as gold, silver, silk, and brocade.[41] It too would have been genteel and objectionable. Gradually, most of the helpers settled on wearing wigs that were simple, nondescript, and conventional.[42]

Their style of living and traveling also was bound to be different from Wesley's. He might follow the genteel mode and spend part of each year in London, part in the country. But they were each assigned by his order to a certain region—or round, as they called it—where they were required to stay for a year, or possibly two or three, at a stretch.[43] A few of them, at least three, managed to afford to keep a personal servant,[44] but most were servantless, except insofar as they might on occasion command one of Wesley's staff, employed at the Methodist society-rooms in the big cities. In the traveling they did within the round, they were not accompanied by a retinue. Usually

[39]Silas Told, *An Account of the Life and Dealings of God with Silas Told, Late Preacher of the Gospel* . . . (London, 1786), p. 88.

[40]O. F. Christie, ed., *Diary of the Rev'd. William Jones, 1777–1821* (London, 1929), pp. 75–76.

[41]Wesley disapproved even of "artificial curls," a relatively unflamboyant wig style. See *Minutes of Conferences*, 1: 157. On the range of styles available to the fashionable, see Janet Arnold, *Perukes and Periwigs* (London, 1970).

[42]Their choice of wigs may be deduced from their pictures in *The Arminian Magazine* from 1778 onward, and from their barber bills. See M. Riggall, "Hairdressers' Charges in Wesley's Time," *Proceedings of the Wesley Historical Society*, 13 (June 1922): 142–43.

[43]Frank Baker, "The People Called Methodists—3. Polity," in Rupert Davies and Gordon Rupp, eds., *A History of the Methodist Church in Great Britain* (London, 1965), 1: 232.

[44]The three known to have kept servants were Samuel Bradburn (a maid), Joseph Benson, and James Rogers. See Eliza Weaver Bradburn, *Memoirs of the late Rev. Samuel Bradburn* . . . (London, 1816), p. 86; James MacDonald, *Memoirs of the Rev. Joseph Benson* (London, 1822), p. 137; and *A Short Account of the Experience of Mrs. Hester Ann Rogers* (New York, 1811), p. 60.

they went alone, sometimes on horseback, and to that extent genteelly (one of them heightened the effect by putting silver stirrups on
his horse),[45] but sometimes on foot. None of them kept a carriage.

In doctoring, too, they could hardly do as Wesley did. He might
advise treatments that he had read about in the medical texts of Her-
mann Boerhaave or Thomas Sydenham; he might learnedly favor
some drugs, like tar-water and "decoction of mallows," and just as
learnedly oppose others, like quinine and quicksilver; he might tell
his poor patients about "obstructed perspiration (vulgarly called
catching cold)" and impress them with a line of talk very nearly
professional.[46] But the helpers, with few exceptions, would know little of Boerhaave and Sydenham. One helper was a physician, and
another a surgeon, and two determinedly read medicine while they
were itinerating;[47] the rest were in no position to give a stunning
impression of medical learning. Still, they ventured to copy Wesley
in treating the sick. They copied him in their own way, as they could.
Instead of trying to play doctor, and failing, they made cure-all med-
icines. They compounded a pill or brewed a "balsam," which they
peddled as they traveled, in the intervals between preaching.[48] But
when Wesley heard of the peddling he forbade it as taking too much
of their time and as undignified,[49] and so barred them from caring for
the sick in the only way they found possible.

Their income was much smaller than Wesley's, and their charity
was necessarily much smaller than his, too. Typically the helpers in
England earned by his order £12 a year. If married, they got an additional sum, and if they had children, a still greater sum. Moreover,
certain of their personal expenses were covered by the societies of the
round where they were stationed.[50] In total value the income of a mar-

---

[45]Atmore, p. 61.

[46]John Wesley, *Primitive Physick: or, An Easy and Natural Method of Curing Most Diseases* (15th ed., corrected and much enlarged; London, 1772), pp. xi, xiv, xv. I quote from the printing designated as no. 15 in Frank Baker, *A Union Catalogue of the Publications of John and Charles Wesley* (Durham, N.C., 1966), p. 76.

[47]John Jones was the physician, George Hudson the surgeon. On Hudson, see "A Friend of Wesley," *Proceedings of the Wesley Historical Society*, 22 (March 1940): 117–18. On the other two, see Atmore, pp. 143, 201. John Whitehead also went to study medicine at the University of Leiden but only after he had stopped itinerating.

[48]Anthony Steele, *History of Methodism in Barnard Castle* (London, 1857), p. 101.

[49]*Minutes of Conferences*, 1: 78–79, 90.

[50]Baker, "People Called Methodists," pp. 234–35.

ried helper with children in, say, 1784, might be £65.[51] That was a tolerable amount. It would have been marginally more, for instance, than the usual income at about the same time of a well-off laborer's family (parents and four children, all six of whom were wage-earners.)[52] But it would have been a tiny fraction of Wesley's income. Nor were the helpers permitted to try to get big sums the way Wesley did, by publishing. He explicitly forbade them to publish anything at a profit to themselves.[53] Two of his helpers had some private means, and four others married women with money;[54] most just lived on what they earned. With comparatively little money at their disposal, then, the helpers could never make the impact in giving that Wesley could. In fact they might have to be careful in handling money, even at the risk of appearing tight. One helper, writing to a Rochdale Methodist, found himself in the unhappy position of having to shift awkwardly from the expression of spiritual wishes to the request: "please to send me the guinea and a half that I lent you."[55]

Dressed in plain blue suits and nondescript wigs, without London season, retinue, or carriage, barred effectively from caring for the sick, without much money to spend or give, the helpers could do little by way of exacting deference. Such authority as they enjoyed among the Methodists was chiefly vicarial. Insofar as they represented Wesley, they might be accepted, even appreciated. But they did not get bows and curtsies.

In fact the flock was inclined to find fault with the helpers, if they asserted themselves in any way whatever. "Arrant coxcombs" was the way a Newcastle man described two of them.[56] A Broadway man characterized another as "wholly unacquainted with that Humble

[51]In 1784 Samuel Bradburn figured his annual income as a helper as between £60 and £70. Bradburn, *Memoirs*, p. 94.

[52]For this estimate, see Gilboy, *Wages in Eighteenth Century England*, pp. 220–21.

[53]*Minutes of Conferences*, 1: 151. Anything *they* might earn publishing was to go into "the common stock."

[54]Atmore, pp. 116, 123, 225, 289, 433. Thomas Olivers was the fourth to marry a woman with money. He had selected his wife in the belief that "the will of God" required that he marry somebody who had "a small competency." Jackson, 1: 227. Some other helpers married women with money but then immediately stopped itinerating. I do not count them here.

[55]George G. Gibbons to Robert Clegg, May 27, 1783, Methodist Archive at the John Rylands University Library of Manchester (hereafter, Methodist Archive).

[56]Joseph Cownley to Christopher Hopper, Dec. 18, 1778, ibid.

mind, that was in Christ."[57] Yet another was so "trying" in his "manner," at least in the view of a Leeds woman, that she was tempted to quit the Methodists altogether.[58] One helper, who was especially disagreeable to the society at Norwich, was actually locked out of the preaching-house one Sunday. But the perpetrators of the lockout eventually accepted "Reproof" and "wrote a penitent acknowledgement of what they had done, to Mr. Wesley."[59]

It was not only in the eyes of the Methodist people that the helpers were subordinate. Parsons and squires looked down on them too. When the helpers preached in the domain of some powerful local figure, especially in the earlier years of the revival, they were in danger, far more so than Wesley could be in the same situation. Wesley might get pushed or clipped with a stone; they ran a much bigger risk. They might get impressed—dragooned into the army or the navy, on the say-so of the local justices of the peace. Wesley was virtually immune from impressment. As a gentleman, a scholar, a fellow of an Oxford college for part of his itinerant career, he could hardly have been disposed of so expeditiously. But the helpers were a different case. They were vulnerable, and at least eight of them were in fact impressed.[60]

In their subordinate position the helpers naturally grumbled, said that Wesley, in his relations with them, was "shackling free-born Englishmen"; that he was determined to be "aut Caesar, aut nihil"; that he was "too full of himself."[61] But they nevertheless agreed—and Whitefield and Charles agreed too—that the success of the revival required Wesley to be elevated, required that he be unapproachably and unimpeachably genteel. On the one occasion when Wesley wanted to risk his status, wanted to risk rendering himself déclassé, they all interfered to stop him.

What happened was that Wesley ventured on a misalliance. He

[57]Unidentified to Charles Wesley, May 22, 1772, ibid.

[58]Joseph Beaumont, *Memoirs of Mrs. Mary Tatham, Late of Nottingham* (New York, 1839), p. 37.

[59]Hodgson manuscript, 1786, Methodist Archive.

[60]Leslie Church, *More About the Early Methodist People* (London, 1949), pp. 82, 83. Church mentions seven who were impressed. An eighth was Thomas Maxfield. Philip Lee, "Thomas Maxfield," *Proceedings of the Wesley Historical Society*, 21 (Sept. 1938): 161–63.

[61]*Minutes of Conferences*, 1: 61; Whitehead, 2: 270; quoted by Curnock, 6: 270.

decided to marry a servant of his, a thirty-two-year-old widow named Grace Murray. She was the housekeeper at the Methodist society-room in Newcastle, and when he took sick while touring the north country in August 1748, she nursed him. He had known her for some ten years already and, as he explained in the little memoir he later wrote concerning their relationship,[62] had long cared for her. While she tended him, his feelings for her grew stronger, he "esteem'd and lov'd her more and more," and he "told her, 'If ever I marry, I think you will be ye Person.'" Once he was recovered, he made her a direct proposal. She answered him, he recalled in his memoir, by saying: "'This is too great a Blessing for me. I can't tell how to believe it.'"[63] From that time he considered that they were engaged. But he gave her to understand that the engagement was to be kept secret; and she may have suspected that it was somehow uncertain, or possibly she may have wanted to escape from him, blessing and all. For as soon as he had parted from her, to go off on a preaching tour, she engaged herself also to another man, one of the helpers, John Bennet.

Whatever she may have felt for Wesley, he certainly felt much for her, "had never before had so strong an Affection for any Person under Heaven," and believed that she would make him an ideal wife. In his memoir he listed her advantages. As a housekeeper she was "remarkably neat" and obeyed all his "Rules," even when he was absent; as a nurse, "indefatigably patient, and unexpressively tender"; as a companion, "mild, sprightly, cheerful, and yet Serious"; as a friend, "faithful"; as a fellow laborer in the gospel, "teachable" and "own'd of God." He noted also that she knew how to reprove him, "if she thought anything amiss" in his conduct, while nevertheless showing him "such deep Esteem and Respect" as he "trembled at, not thinking it was the due of any Creature."[64]

She informed Wesley by letter of her engagement to Bennet. The news did not stop him. He summoned her, as his servant, to accompany him on a preaching tour of Ireland, and once she was in his presence, got her to agree that because the engagement to Bennet had

[62]This memoir Wesley never published. It came out posthumously. I quote from the best available edition: J. A. Leger, *John Wesley's Last Love* (London, 1910).
[63]Leger, p. 1.
[64]Ibid., pp. 70–74.

come second, it was not "binding." Their own engagement was still secret. But they spent several months together traveling in Ireland. He preached, and she acted as his "Servant and Friend as well as Fellow-labourer in ye Gospel."[65]

In 1749 they returned to England, stopping for a while at Bristol and London before heading north to Lancashire. There Bennet intercepted them and claimed Grace Murray as his own. For some days she veered between her two suitors. At last she chose Wesley, and together they rode to Newcastle. After they had arrived there he wrote Bennet a letter of reproof. As a helper Bennet was supposed to do "nothing of importance," the letter said, without first consulting Wesley. Yet acting quite independently, he had asked a woman to marry him. That was wrong, and to ask this particular woman was a further wrong. It was to try "to rob" Wesley of the "faithful Servant, of ye Fellow-labourer in ye Gospel whom he had been forming to his hand for ten years."[66] Wesley gave the letter to William Shent, another of his helpers, and told him to deliver it personally to Bennet. He mailed a copy of it to his brother Charles, then in Bristol.

That Wesley wanted to marry one of his servants was no longer a secret. Charles got notice of it by way of the copy of the letter to Bennet. Those in Lancashire who had been around while the woman had been veering between her two suitors also knew. Those in Newcastle who had seen Wesley arrive with the woman and had observed his manners to her could guess. And wherever in Methodist circles the news of the projected marriage spread, there was consternation and there was anger.

Shent kept the letter, did not deliver it to Bennet. Charles, deeply shocked and certain that Wesley's marrying a servant would "put a stop to ye work of God," rushed from Bristol to Leeds, where he conferred with Whitefield and several of the helpers, and then on to Newcastle. At Newcastle he was told that the rumor of the marriage had put the city "in an uproar," and that "all ye Societies" in the vicinity were "ready to fly in pieces." He then rode to Whitehaven, where his brother had lately gone on a new preaching tour. There the two of them met, and Charles spoke pointedly. He said, Wesley re-

---

[65] Ibid., pp. 4–5.
[66] Ibid., pp. 9–14. Here Wesley was strenuously candid, for during part of those ten years, Grace Murray had been married to somebody else, her first husband.

called in his memoir, that all the "Preachers wd leave" and all the "Societies disperse," if Wesley "married so mean a woman." Her involvement with Bennet he spoke of as yet another scandal. Next morning he spoke again and so much "more warmly" that Wesley left and went out for a walk by himself.[67] While Wesley was out Charles determined to act. He took horse and set off for the farmhouse where Grace Murray was staying. Arriving the following day, he kissed her, told her, " 'Grace Murray, you have broke my heart,' " and, overcome by emotion, fell to the floor. Afterwards he got up, talked some more, and persuaded her to ride away with him. When Wesley arrived at the farmhouse two hours later, he found that they were both gone, and said, " 'The Lord gave, and ye Lord hath taken away.' " He did not pursue them but instead continued preaching through the countryside, feeling occasionally, he said in his memoir, some "Heaviness," and dreaming once of Grace Murray being executed and of her face turning black.[68]

Meanwhile Charles carried Grace off to another farmhouse, left her, and rode into Newcastle, where he conferred again with several of the helpers and with Whitefield, lately arrived there too.[69] No record of any sort exists of what they said among themselves.[70] It may reasonably be assumed that they agreed that the threat of Wesley's marrying Grace Murray and wrecking the revival could be averted, if she were quickly married to John Bennet. For the upshot of their talk was that efforts to reconcile Murray and Bennet were begun immediately. These efforts took only five days. Charles had arrived in Newcastle on September 28; Bennet and Murray were married at the Church of St. Andrew on the morning of October 3. Meantime Whitefield was commissioned to write to Wesley, still on tour, and tell him to be sure to keep his preaching appointment in Leeds on October 4, so that the three of them, Wesley, Charles, and Whitefield, could all meet there on that day. This letter was probably intended to decoy him away from Newcastle, where the wedding was about to take place.

[67]Ibid., pp. 64–65, 79; *A Select Collection of the Letters of the Late George Whitefield* (London, 1772), 2: 282. Leger, pp. 65, 65–66, 79.
[68]Leger, pp. 81, 84, 90.
[69]*Select Collection*, 2: 283.
[70]John Bennet's journal in the Methodist Archive is blank for this period.

Although the letter specified that Charles and Whitefield both would see Wesley in Leeds on the fourth, only Whitefield set out to meet him and deal with him there. Charles remained at Newcastle to make sure the marriage was performed.[71] At the time Bennet and Murray were speaking their vows, Wesley was safely out of the way, traveling toward Old-Hutton, on the road to Leeds. When he arrived there on the night of the fourth, he found just Whitefield, already in bed. Wesley must have expected bad news; he lay down next to Whitefield, who told him at once that Charles "wd not come, till J. B. and G. M. were married." Wesley felt, he later said in his memoir, "troubled,"[72] and Whitefield tried hard to provide comfort. He spoke agreeably to Wesley's feelings, said that Wesley did have a prior claim on Grace Murray, that their wedding perhaps ought to have been postponed until Wesley could have talked with all the persons involved, that Charles had been impetuous. After this comfort, and despite his disappointment and pain, Wesley at last fell asleep.

In the memoir he tried to justify his conduct throughout the affair and to refute the view that Charles had expressed at Whitehaven, that his marrying so lowborn a woman as Grace Murray would have destroyed the Methodist movement. That her parents were "poor, Labouring people," he acknowledged. But he denied that her origin was important. What mattered was that she had grace and gifts. "Besides," he added, "whoever I marry, I believe it will not be a Gentlewoman; I despair of finding any such, so qualified." That she was a

[71]It is just possible that both Charles and Whitefield remained to make sure that the marriage was performed, and that Whitefield rushed to Leeds immediately after. See William Bennet, *Memoirs of Mrs. Grace Bennet* (Macclesfield, 1803), p. 19.

[72]Leger, p. 87. Frank Baker supposes that Wesley and Grace Murray were already married under the terms of the then-existing law. They had married just by the exchange of promises "de praesenti." If Wesley had wished, Baker says, he could have sued to try to have the marriage recognized and to have the Bennet-Murray union declared bigamous. By refraining from suing, Wesley was in effect agreeing to the dissolution of the marriage he had made with Murray. For the law provided also that a marriage based just on the exchange of promises, and unconsummated, could be dissolved by mutual consent. Frank Baker, "John Wesley's First Marriage," *London Quarterly and Holborn Review*, 192 (Oct. 1967): 305–15. Baker is right about the provisions of the law of marriage. What he fails to see is that Bennet and Murray could have alleged (and proved with evidence as good or as bad as Wesley and Murray had) a prior exchange of promises "de praesenti." Had Wesley sued, no court would have found for him. He never married Grace Murray.

servant, his own servant, he also acknowledged. But he denied that her employment with him should have been an impediment to marriage. It was in fact an advantage. Because she had lived so long under his roof, he could know on the basis of experience that she was trustworthy. "Indeed," he said, "I shd scruple marrying any Woman, who had not done so for some time." That she had traveled with him for several months, and that some people would probably suppose that she had been his mistress, he acknowledged too; but he was used to such malicious gossip, and it did no real harm. All together, he was sure that these arguments of his, if "fairly represented," would have satisfied "nineteen in twenty" of the helpers and societies.[73]

An additional consideration that would have made the marriage peculiarly eligible was that it would have brought little "increase of expense." In marrying a servant he would have been assuming financial responsibility for somebody he was already maintaining anyway. After the marriage she presumably would have wanted "nothing more than she had before," and would have consented "cheerfully" that the children of the union, if any, "be wholly brought up at Kingswood," the Methodist school.[74]

So ran the case that Wesley urged anxiously in self-justification: the marriage could have been explained to nineteen in twenty of the helpers and societies. Whatever they might have felt at his marrying a servant of plebeian origins, who had moreover traveled in his employ for some months, could have been argued away. He did not name, and possibly could not have named, anybody in the movement who agreed with him. That Charles and Whitefield and the helpers disagreed, they had shown by their quick and concerted action. In their view his marrying Grace Murray would have cost him what the success of the revival in part depended on, his perfect and well-played gentility. Only somebody who is credibly a master gets bows and curtsies.

[73]Leger, pp. 76–79.
[74]Ibid., p. 69.

Chapter Three

The Basis of
Wesley's Influence:
Love

Wesley could influence plebeians first, then, because of his success in playing the gentleman and exacting deference. On the one occasion that he misplayed the role and risked rendering himself déclassé, his colleagues intervened and stopped him, for the sake of "ye work of God." But important as this success was in producing his influence, it would never have been alone sufficient. Deference, among eighteenth-century English plebeians, was impermanent, "brittle";[1] it could easily break and turn into resistance or riot. Wesley did more than just exact deference; he also won love.

Each of the conventional deference-inducing counters of genteel behavior he used in a special and original way so as to win love too. First, his appearance, his dress and grooming, was conventionally genteel, but he managed it with a difference. He took himself and his ensemble, the gown, the cassock, the bands, the gold, the silver, the brocade, the silk, the beautiful hair, directly to the poor, to their places of work and recreation, to the quay at Robin Hood's Bay, to a meadow at St. Ives, to a brickyard at Bristol, to the house where the lead miners were getting paid at Blanchland, to the copperworks near the Hayle, to the High Street at Stockton, to the common at Portsmouth.[2] He got close to them, on their own ground, and the closeness was unexpected coming from a gentleman so fine as he was.

[1] Here I follow E. P. Thompson, "Patrician Society, Plebeian Culture," *Journal of Social History*, 7 (Summer 1974), especially p. 399.

[2] Nehemiah Curnock, ed., *The Journal of the Rev. John Wesley, A.M.* (London, 1909–16), 4: 223; 5: 381; 2: 172; 3: 364; 7: 110; 4: 65, 83.

Typically they reacted by getting close to him, too, by crowding around, partly from curiosity, possibly still more from a quick wish to reciprocate his move toward them. While they gathered, he would usually mount a makeshift pulpit, a "horseblock" maybe, or a table,[3] give out a hymn, and begin to preach or exhort. Listening, they would continue to notice his fineness, and some might want to feel that he was reaching out to them individually. As a Yorkshireman wrote, describing the "blessed morning" when he had first heard Wesley preach, "Soon as he got upon the stand, he stroked back his hair, and turned his face towards where I stood, and I thought fixed his eyes on me."[4] Even if the hearers were inclined to be hostile, Wesley's presence there among them, dressed and groomed as he was, might still be peculiarly attractive. Once, for instance, he got caught at Darlaston in an angry crowd. A man rushed forward raising his arm "to strike," as Wesley noted in his Journal, but then stopped abruptly and just "stroked" Wesley's head, saying, "What soft hair he has!"[5]

His style of living and traveling was also genteel with a difference. He kept London lodgings, yet far from the center of fashion at Piccadilly and St. James, and relatively near to most of his flock on the south and east sides of the city.[6] Although he followed the genteel mode and spent part of every year at these lodgings, he timed his stay there very much in his own way. For the great world, the London season closed in early June, and March or perhaps early April was the choicest part of all.[7] It was then that London was most fashionably active. But every year before the season had closed, before it had even peaked, Wesley left town to make a long tour of the countryside. He left usually at the very start of March and so gave to the poor whom he traveled to see even the time the genteel liked best to reserve for each other.

Wesley varied the pattern of genteel living and traveling in an-

[3]Ibid., 3: 98; 4: 442.
[4]John Nelson, *The Journal of Mr. John Nelson, Preacher of the Gospel* . . . (London, 1846), p. 13.
[5]Curnock, 3: 101.
[6]First he lived at Moorfields, then on City Road. West End society regarded the architecture in Wesley's neighborhood as vulgar. John Summerson, *Georgian London* (rev. ed.; London, 1962), pp. 58–59.
[7]H. J. Habakkuk, "England," in A. Goodwin, ed., *The European Nobility in the Eighteenth Century* (rev. ed.; New York, 1967), p. 4.

other, still more important, way. When the genteel left London and traveled to the country, they traveled usually to their own family house set on their own land. If they had no such house, then they hoped to have one eventually. But Wesley neither had a country place nor took any steps to get one; nor did he show any signs of wanting one. When he traveled to the country he usually offered himself to his flock as a guest. Gentleman though he was, he asked for their hospitality. He ate at their tables and slept under their roofs. Often the accommodations were rough. He might find that he was obliged to share a bed with another man or sleep in a cellar,[8] and the food might be plain. Still, Wesley stayed with them, and they adored him for allowing them to host him.

It is true that there were some hardships that he refused to bear. He was unwilling, for instance, to sleep in the same room as a married couple, and when once he was offered such an accommodation at a house in Cornwall, he declined it and traveled some way farther until he could find another.[9] Nor would he stay anyplace that lacked a "necessary house."[10] And although he would take plain food, he expected his hosts to give him their best. Almost always they did. But if they did not, he would complain. Once on tour, again in Cornwall, he got served a meal of just bread and cheese, and he was so irritated by the slight that he reproached his hosts in his published Journal. He wrote that obviously they would not be "ruined" by "entertaining" him "once a year."[11]

Even when he encountered none of the hardships he felt as unbearable, he still must have found the work of staying with his flock tiring. For on occasion he would slip away and stay with a gentry family instead—personal acquaintances or sympathizers. At their houses he could rest, could sink back into an atmosphere of relative comfort. But in slipping away to such gentry acquaintances or sympathizers, Wesley always risked hurting the Methodists, who had learned to hope for the chance to accommodate him. Once at Banff,

---

[8]Curnock, 3: 346; 4: 32.

[9]Ibid., 4: 238.

[10]John Telford, ed., *The Letters of the Rev. John Wesley, A.M.* (London, 1931), 5: 134.

[11]Ibid., 3: 379. Wesley only leveled this reproach in the first edition of his Journal. In all the other editions published during his lifetime, he omitted it.

in Scotland, he left the society members after the preaching and went off to stay at great houses for two days in succession. Seven months later the Methodists of Banff still felt wounded at his desertion. Two of them, a married couple, wrote jointly to one of the helpers, describing the state of the society. They said, "We are often neglected," and then wrote on, unable fully to express their hurt or fully to hide it:

Lately we had only one visit in eight weeks. Mr. Wesley was here on 20th May last, and preached on the Parade from 2 Cor. VIII. 9. He supped at Lord Banff's and next night at Admiral Gordon's lady's house, with a great number of great ones; and at their request, he preached in the English chapel to an elegant and crowded congregation.[12]

Wesley gave as few occasions as he could for this kind of mute hurt. As he traveled he stayed mostly with his flock and let them take care of him. They in turn treasured the privilege. One Methodist, a Whitehaven bootmaker, whose cottage Wesley had stayed at, kept the bed he had used inviolate ever after, allowing nobody else to sleep there; and at the bootmaker's death another Methodist eagerly bought the bed.[13]

Wesley also doctored with a difference. He treated the usual run of somatic complaints, ague, fever, consumption, but he concerned himself too with what he called "nervous" diseases. He would care for a man suffering from "lowness of spirits" or for a woman wracked by "continual pain in her stomach," caused as he thought by her "fretting for the death of her son."[14] For such nervous diseases he prescribed prayer, and as he could, as he had the time, provided also person-to-person pastoral guidance. But starting in 1756 he used another remedy as well. It was a remedy that was cheap and quick, and it could be prescribed on a mass basis. It was electricity.

Wesley had read of Benjamin Franklin's experiments, had heard also of a few instances of electric shock being used as part of a medical regimen, and he was intrigued by the potentialities of the newly available medium. Person-to-person help he could provide to rela-

[12]Quoted by Luke Tyerman, *The Life and Times of the Rev. John Wesley, A.M.* (2d ed.; London, 1870–72), 3: 225. Here as elsewhere Tyerman prints manuscripts that are apparently no longer extant.
[13]G. H. B. Judge, "Methodism in Whitehaven," *Proceedings of the Wesley Historical Society*, 19 (March 1933), 27–28.
[14]Curnock, 2: 241; 4: 313.

tively few of the nervous among his numerous and ever-growing flock. Electricity he could give everybody. For the apparatus that produced it was simple, cost little to make, and could be used anytime, anywhere, by any sufferer, without Wesley's immediate supervision. He started slowly, experimentally, setting up at first just a single apparatus at the London society-room, and appointing "some hours in every week" when "any that desired it might try the virtue of this surprising medicine." Soon the users were so many that he let them come "an hour in every day." Then, soon after that, he set up apparatuses at three other London locations to serve still more sufferers.[15] From London the electricity-cure spread to Methodist societies throughout the kingdom. By the late 1780's there was an apparatus even on the Isle of Jersey.[16]

To use the apparatus was easy. It was just a machine with two wires attached. If the patient's symptom was, for instance, a "palsy of the tongue" (stuttering, or some other speech defect, or maybe a hysterical inability to speak), then the shock would be administered "by applying one wire to the hinder part of the neck, and another to the tongue." If he or she had an "ague in the head" (a migraine headache), both wires would be applied to the skull.[17] Wesley's physician-contemporaries were skeptical about the electricity-cure,[18] but his patients were overwhelmingly satisfied, and he viewed it ever more confidently. In the little guidebook he wrote concerning it, about four years after he had set up his first apparatus, he recommended it for a wide range of diseases, but especially for diseases "of the nervous kind," including "epilepsy," "hysterics," "contractions of the limbs," and "knots in the flesh."[19] He ventured to say that perhaps any "nervous distemper whatever" would "yield to a steady use of this remedy," and that certainly more of them could be cured by it "in one

[15] Ibid., p. 190.

[16] James Everett, *Adam Clarke Portrayed* (London, 1843), 2: 26.

[17] [John Wesley], *The Desideratum: Or Electricity Made Plain and Useful* (3d ed.; London, 1790), pp. 43, 71. I am quoting here from the printing designated as 3 in Frank Baker, *A Union Catalogue of the Publications of John and Charles Wesley* (Durham, N.C., 1966), p. 112.

[18] A. Wesley Hill, *John Wesley Among the Physicians* (London, 1958), p. 87. But see Roy Porter, *Mind Forg'd Manacles* (Cambridge, Mass., 1987), p. 185.

[19] Wesley, *Desideratum*, pp. 42–43.

year" than "the whole English Materia Medica" could cure until "the end of the century."[20]

Apparently the Methodists used electricity as commonly and readily as Wesley wished. Even when they were feeling just "low-spirited," they might stop at an apparatus to get a couple of shocks.[21] To Wesley, the source of this release, this stimulus, they responded as "nervous" patients usually do to those who treat them. They responded with love.[22] Sometimes the love was exceedingly dependent. On at least one occasion he found a Methodist who yearned for him to cure her thaumaturgically, by touch alone. She had been suffering for four weeks from a bad pain in the head and thought that if he would lay his hand on her cheek, she would recover. She asked him to do so; he complied; and from that moment she felt no more pain.[23]

Wesley gave charity with a difference too. In genteel society there were strict though largely tacit conventions governing giving. Every gentleman of means was thought to be responsible for preserving his estate. He was supposed to provide or bequeath something substantial to those closest to him, something at least as good as he had got himself. To fail to do so was reason for the deepest censure. Any charitable giving he might do, or any spending, was to be limited by that overarching responsibility. So if a gentleman "lived to 90 years," with many "opportunities of saving for his children," but nevertheless left at his death only £2,000, then he would probably be regarded by his own set as a disgrace. In letters and in conversation he might be stigmatized, sneered at, called a "vicious, expensive man."[24]

But that was only half of the code. If to accumulate too little in

[20]Ibid., pp. vi–vii. For pertinent background of various kinds, see Porter, *Mind*, passim; and Michael MacDonald, "Religion, Social Change, and Psychological Healing in England, 1600–1800," in W. J. Shiels, ed., *The Church and Healing* (Oxford, 1982), pp. 101–25.

[21]James Chubb journal, June 3, 1780, Methodist Archive.

[22]It is by no means just psychoanalysts who get this response from "nervous" patients. As Freud noted, all therapists do. "The Dynamics of Transference," in James Strachey et al., eds., *Standard Edition of the Complete Psychological Works of Sigmund Freud* (London, 1954–66), 12: 101.

[23]Curnock, 7: 86.

[24]Albert Hartshorne, ed., *Memoirs of a Royal Chaplain, 1729–1763* (London, 1905), p. 325.

relation to income was disgraceful, to accumulate too much was equally bad. Every gentleman was supposed to be liberal in disposing of money, in giving it away and in spending it too. His spending could be entirely according to his taste, and there were also many options for his charity. He might, for example, dispense at times of dearth "a whole copper full of broth," thickened "with oatmeal or blue pease," or at Christmas, "bread and lincloth," or during freezing weather, coal, or at no particular time of the year, for no particular reason, cash money, say, £6, conveyed by servants and intended to be doled out in portions to about 110 people.[25] Whatever the form of his spending and giving, he would have to do both freely. Otherwise he would probably be despised. To say of somebody genteel that he had accumulated much money in relation to his income was to attack him. Take the reaction of one clergyman to a story in a London newspaper reporting that the Bishop of Salisbury had left behind him a huge estate valued at £150,000. Immediately the clergyman assumed that the story was a smear put about by "Dissenters and Deists to belie and bespatter the Church of England." To believe that the bishop had amassed "so much wealth" was impossible. For he had "always lived like a Gentleman" and had never been known for "Avarice."[26]

These, then, were the conventions: every gentleman was supposed to provide or accumulate for those closest to him, but to spend and give freely while doing so. For one of substantial means £2,000 might be far too little to leave behind, £150,000 far too much. It is interesting to note in this connection that the bishops of the Church of England tended to leave behind a properly intermediate amount. £8,600 was the approximate median value of the estates of those whose wills were proved between 1722 and 1760.[27] Wesley broke all the conventions. He accumulated *nothing*; he gave away all that he earned except what he wanted for his day-to-day expenses. He bought no plate, put no money out at interest, invested no money in land. He made

[25] F. J. Manning, ed., *The Williamson Letters* (Bedford, 1954), p. 14; W. Brockbank and F. Kenworthy, eds., *Diary of Richard Kay, 1716–51, of Baldingstone near Bury* (Manchester, 1968), p. 40; *Extracts from the Leeds Mercury, 1737–1742* (Leeds, 1919–22), p. 82; C. E. Whiting, ed., *Two Yorkshire Diaries* (Leeds, 1952), p. 145.

[26] Francis Griffin Stokes, ed., *Blecheley Diary of the Rev. William Cole, 1765–1767* (London, 1931), pp. 52–53.

[27] D. Hirschberg, "A Social History of the Anglican Episcopate" (Ph.D. dissertation, University of Michigan, 1976), p. 415.

no settlements on his stepchildren, gave no portions to his nieces and nephews, bequeathed no fortune to anybody; and to make sure that the Methodists knew the strange extent of his charity, knew that he was giving them virtually everything he got, he told them so again and again, on every possible public occasion, in his polemical pamphlets, in his letters, and especially in the Journal that he published periodically. Once, for instance, when he was sick, probably with pleurisy, and thought he was dying, he even wrote himself an epitaph. He survived the sickness but saved the epitaph, and because it made the point he wanted to make, he inserted it in the installment of the Journal that he brought out some years after:[28]

Here lieth the Body
of
John Wesley
A Brand Plucked Out of the Burning:
Who Died of a Consumption in the Fifty-first Year of His Age,
Not leaving, after his debts are paid,
Ten pounds behind him . . .

Naturally the Methodists responded to a charity so unconventionally wide and so firmly pointed out to them. They felt for him lovingly, as for a parent, and liked to call him, not brother, in the usual Protestant style, but "Our good old father."[29]

Wesley's charity was unconventionally wide in another sense too. He offered more than just money. He offered something that was deeply valued, and had long been deeply valued, in the culture of the plebeians to whom he preached. He offered salvation, and he offered it to all of them, none excepted. This charity he called by the clear and appropriate name "free grace."[30] He set no limit to the number who might avail themselves of it, denied that any set group, so big and no bigger, had been elected from eternity to have it, and required of those who wanted it only, at first, that they repent and believe.

---

[28]Curnock, 4: 90. For another instance of his mentioning his charity, see ibid., 7: 462. At some point Wesley may have even given away a pair of his silver buckles. See Frederick Gill, *In the Steps of John Wesley* (London, 1962), p. 53.

[29]Curnock, 6: 18.

[30]John Wesley, *Free Grace: A Sermon Preach'd at Bristol* (4th ed.; London, 1754), esp. p. 4. I quote from the printing designated as 4 in Baker, *Union Catalogue*, p. 25.

Wesley's offer troubled his fellow clergymen of the Church of England. It sounded to them "not guarded."[31] But many of the Methodists who closed with his offer recalled afterward how important the universality of it had been to them. For their self-esteem was in many ways low. They could believe that salvation was possible for them only if they were continually assured that it was available on easy terms to everybody. One London man acknowledged that he owed his "all" to the preaching of free grace, and a London woman explained in a letter about her spiritual state that she found she was most "Quicken'd and Strengthen'd" when the hymns on free grace were sung.[32] To Wesley, who made them the "not-guarded" offer that meant so much, the Methodists were lovingly grateful, and they showed what they felt. Wesley recorded in his Journal that as he spoke, for instance, at Gateshead, the poor roughly clothed children who gathered around looked at him yearningly, "as if they would have swallowed" him up, especially, he added, while he was "applying" these words, "Be it known unto you, men and brethren, that through this man is preached unto you forgiveness of sins."[33]

Wesley handled the usual counters of genteel conduct, then, so as not only to exact deference but also to win love. He dressed and groomed himself as a gentleman but stepped out of his own set, went directly to the poor, to their own ground, and let them hear him there, see him, and even on occasion stroke him. He kept London lodgings, but in a dissonantly unfashionable part of town near his flock, and annually left for the country before the season had peaked. In the country he had no place of his own, no estate. He stayed with his flock, let them feed him and house him. He provided medical care without charge wherever he went, but took an especially keen interest in the kind of patients who responded most emotionally to their healer and treated them by a cheap, quick method of his own that enabled him to care easily for as many thousands as came his way. He gave money in charity, but far more in proportion to his income than other gentlemen, even clerical gentlemen, considered right or proper. This charity he advertised carefully, and he capped it with a

---

[31]Curnock, 2: 321. These were the words of an Exeter clergyman. He conceded, however, that Wesley's preaching was doctrinally correct.

[32]George Stevenson, *City Road Chapel, London, and Its Associations* (London, n.d.), p. 345; Elizabeth Sais to Charles Wesley, May 1742, Methodist Archive.

[33]Curnock, 3: 69.

charity still greater and more important to his hearers: he offered them all free grace.

In return they loved him. As he traveled and preached, he observed their affection. At Barnard Castle he found a "simple, loving, earnest people"; at St. John's, a "loving, earnest people"; at Colchester, a "poor, loving, simple-hearted people"; at Ely, "a plain, loving people."[34] Sometimes they were especially demonstrative, as once at Newcastle, where the men, women, and children all "hung" upon him so that he could hardly disengage himself; at St. Ives, where he was surprised to hear himself welcomed by a loud "cry"; at Athlone, in Ireland, where after the preaching, he would have dismissed the flock, but "none seemed willing to go," for they wanted to continue just looking at him.[35]

When he was absent, preaching elsewhere, they continued to love him. They prayed for him, of course, and perhaps with particular pleasure. One Macclesfield woman recorded in her diary: "I had a good time in Private, especially in interceding for D[ea]r Mr. Wesley."[36] A London woman prayed that she might be found at his "feet" on the "day of the Lord."[37] Not only did they pray for him; they also yearned for him, particularly when they were unwell. One woman hallucinated in the course of a fever that she was with him, and a man begged, in anticipation of death, that Wesley preach at his funeral.[38]

Despite their love for him they sometimes misbehaved, showed themselves refractory to his rules, stubborn, willful. At such times he would repeat his rules, would chide and warn them, and then, if they were still misbehaving, he would level his ultimate threat. He would say, do as I tell you, or "you will see my face no more."[39]

Just as Wesley had to compete for the deference of the plebeians, so too he competed for their love. Here the struggle was just with his

[34]Ibid., 5: 68, 338; 6: 5, 51.
[35]Ibid., 3: 60, 127, 483.
[36]Hester Roe Rogers journal, Methodist Archive.
[37]Curnock, 4: 167.
[38]Ibid., p. 206; 3: 199.
[39]Ibid., 7: 232. "This," he said, "struck deep." For another instance of his use of the threat, see ibid., 4: 76. Wesley was oddly echoing Paul's words to the elders of Ephesus in Acts 20:25: "And now, behold, I know that ye all, among whom I have gone preaching the Kingdom of God, shall see my face no more."

fellow evangelists, and the victory was relatively easy. It is true that Charles, during the early years of the revival, proved almost as attractive as Wesley himself. But after marrying in 1749, Charles gradually desisted from traveling and spent more and more time at home (first Bristol, then later London), raising a big family, writing hymns, and preaching to the local flock. The Methodists elsewhere rarely saw him. Whitefield, after 1740, devoted himself as much to America as to England. Besides, he died early. He was felled by "asthma" at Newburyport, Massachusetts, in 1770; Wesley preached the memorial sermon in London and lived for another twenty-one years.

As for the helpers, they were less effective competitors than Charles or Whitefield. Since they wore no genteel ensemble, their physical presence as they preached at markets or innyards was in no way special. Nobody reached out to stroke their hair. Like Wesley they let the flock feed them and house them, but their availability was felt more as a burden than as a delight. It was clear enough that they wanted free accommodation because they could afford nothing else. Wesley, in accepting hospitality, conferred on his hosts an extraordinary favor; the helpers took what they could hardly have done without. As a result the flock often grumbled about the expense of entertaining them. At Darwen they were all called by the nickname "Owd Preach-for-Bacon."[40]

Except for the handful who were medically trained, the helpers were no more prepared to talk a lively line on nervous disease than on any other kind. Besides, Wesley disqualified them from making an effort in that direction. He stigmatized them publicly as *suffering* in disproportionate numbers from nervous disease, caused, he explained, by their "indolence" and "intemperance."[41] Finally, they might give their all in charity and still give very little; and offers of free grace from them were naturally felt as less generous and less reassuring than those that came from so elevated a figure as Wesley.

For all these reasons the helpers were in a much less favorable position for winning love than Wesley was. But even if they somehow succeeded in building a tender relationship with the flock of their

[40]James Townsend, *History of Darwen Wesleyan Methodism* (Rossendale and Stockport, 1916), pp. 23–24.
[41]*Minutes of the Methodist Conferences* (London, 1862), 1: 130.

round, the relationship was bound to be short-lived. Wesley permitted them to remain in a round for only a certain set time. Then he moved them to another round, and they might never again see the flock they had served before. Only Wesley himself toured the rounds every year, as many as he could manage, year after year. Only Wesley returned again and again and again.

Prevented from winning love as Wesley won it, the helpers sometimes tried a simpler means. They fondled the flock or kissed them or even, on occasion, took them to bed.[42] If Wesley found out he expelled them from the connection. But the fact is, they were trying to copy him. They were practicing a kind of seduction they could manage successfully, instead of a kind they could not.

That the Methodists loved Wesley, actually loved him, was apparent to all contemporary observers. Those who felt suspicious of him, or hostile, typically assumed that he was behaving like the fallen helpers, flirting, kissing, fondling, taking the flock to bed with him. Sometimes the gossip surfaced in the press, as for instance in a story concerning "the tête-à-tête" between "the Pious Preacher"—plainly, from the context, Wesley—and "Miss D——mple."[43] Sometimes the gossip took a more destructive form, as when the Bishop of Exeter

---

[42] At least two helpers did so: James Wheatley and Westley Hall. See Curnock, 3: 327, 531–33. Three, if Roger Ball be considered a helper. See ibid., 3: 463. (There were possibly more. Over the years many helpers were expelled. Their offenses were never specified in the printed record, so one cannot be sure just what the charges were. See *Minutes of Conferences*, passim.) It was this sort of behavior on the part of some of the helpers that gave rise to the many jokes and double entendres current in eighteenth-century conversation and literature about preaching seductionists. Perhaps the best are to be found in Smollett's masterpiece *Humphrey Clinker*, where Tabitha Bramble, the evangelical spinster, writes to her maid about Clinker, a young preacher who has already done wonders for one woman, by laboring "exceedingly, that she may bring forth fruits of repentance." Tabitha continues: "I make no doubt that he will take the same pains with that pert hussey Mary Jones, and all of you; and that he may have the power to penetrate and instill his goodness, even into your most inward parts, is the fervent prayer of, Your friend in the spirit, Tab. Bramble." Tobias Smollett, *The Expedition of Humphrey Clinker*, ed. H. M. Jones (London, 1943), p. 262. For some other instances of such jokes, see Peter Paragraph, *The Methodist and Mimick* (2d ed.; London, 1767), p. 12; and Christopher Anstey, *New Bath Guide* (4th ed.; London, 1767), pp. 134–36.

[43] *Town and Country Magazine, or Universal Repository of Knowledge, Instruction, and Entertainment.* Supplement to the Year 1774, p. 681.

told his clergy, during his visitation in 1749, that he had heard that Wesley had tried to seduce a maid at an inn at Mitchel.[44] Wesley usually ignored the stories that surfaced in the press. But he felt obliged to do something about what the Bishop of Exeter had said, and in August 1750 he stopped at the inn at Mitchel where the rumor must have originated. Here he spoke to the landlady, who testified in front of the two witnesses whom he had brought along that she had never told anybody that Wesley had been "rude" with the maid.[45] When he returned to London in November, he wrote to the bishop, repeating the substance of his interview with the landlady and in effect demanding a retraction. None was forthcoming. So far from retracting the rumor, the bishop later repeated it in print under his own signature, although without committing himself definitely on whether or not he thought it true.[46]

After writing to the bishop, Wesley decided to try to stop the gossip altogether. He decided once again to try to marry. He made this decision in 1751, some seventeen months after Charles and Whitefield and the helpers had stepped between him and Grace Murray. This time he proceeded prudently. He chose a woman of standing, Molly Vazeille, a banker's widow with a fortune of about £10,000 and a house in London on Threadneedle Street. But since even she was a woman more of fortune than birth, and just moderately genteel, Wesley feared that his colleagues might again interfere for the sake of "ye work of God." To be sure of getting her, he kept his plans to himself and married her privately.[47]

Doubtless Wesley wanted a wife. By then he was forty-eight years old, had never been married, had never enjoyed any regular and sanctioned access to sexual intimacy with another person. But the point he emphasized in justifying the marriage to his followers was that it would stop the continuous gossip about him. Nobody would talk of him anymore as a bachelor rake. Newspaper stories about tête-à-têtes,

[44]Telford, *Letters*, 3: 46.
[45]Ibid.; Curnock, 3: 492.
[46]*The Bishop of Exeter's Answer to Mr. J. Wesley's Late Letter to His Lordship* (London, 1752), pp. 9, 12.
[47]So as far as I know, no documentary record of this marriage has ever been found, though whole cohorts of Methodist antiquaries have searched. It was probably clandestine. At the time clandestine marriages were canonically irregular but legal.

episcopal rumormongering: all that would end. He said that the marriage would make him more useful in the revival movement, that it would serve to remove "the prejudice about the world and him."[48]

In fact the marriage accomplished nothing of the sort. The gossip, the suspicions, continued as before, with just this difference: that now his wife joined in them. Previously she had been on the fringes of the Methodist movement. Now she observed close up the love that his followers felt for him, and like many others, she could account for a love so deep only on the supposition that Wesley was misbehaving sexually. She grew fretful and jealous, opened his mail, spied on him, forbade him to meet his women followers in private, beat him, and eventually, after seven years of marriage, left him. Sometime shortly before their separation, John Hampson, one of the helpers, walked into a room where she was beating Wesley. As Hampson later described the scene, Wesley was sprawled out on the floor, and she had hold of his hair and was pulling him, dragging him, trying to tear it out by the roots.[49]

So the love that Wesley won from his followers caused him much trouble. It sparked gossip; it wrecked his marriage with Mrs. Vazeille; and it also prompted in him some measure of self-doubt. For he could never be sure that he was right to win so much love. He did not accuse himself of sexual misbehavior, as the press, the bishop, and his wife did. Here his conscience was clear. What worried him was something different. It was the thought that he might be monopolizing his followers' love, might be absorbing it totally, might be drawing it to himself instead of channeling it to God. According to conventional Protestant doctrine, he was entitled to some measure of

---

[48]Curnock, 3: 515.

[49]Tyerman, *Life and Times*, 2: 110. It is worth noting that Wesley had often tried to get his wife to defer to him but had usually failed. During the course of one of their quarrels, for instance, he had written to her to warn her against disobeying him, for, as he said in closing, "every act of disobedience is an act of rebellion against God and the King as well as against, Your affectionate husband." Telford, *Letters*, 4: 89. Why had he failed with her, while succeeding with the Methodists? One reason may be that marriages among the well-to-do were tending to "open" during the eighteenth century, that wives were resisting and husbands losing command, at least in some measure. See Lawrence Stone, *The Family, Sex, and Marriage in England, 1500–1800* (New York, 1977), especially pp. 221, 224.

love from his flock.[50] But to eclipse God in their hearts would be disastrously wrong.

From the very earliest days of the revival, he preached to them anxiously, insistently, about the love of God. One Methodist heard him on this subject in a barn filled with "Cotigers," and recorded in his journal that Wesley had preached especially well, had "laid all his greatness aside," and had suited his remarks to the capacity of his hearers. He had begun by telling them that love was the way to heaven. Then he had "interogated the people, by saying: 'But you will say, how can we know when we love God?'" By way of answering this question, he had asked some others, rhetorically: "'I ask you, men, how do you know when you love your wives? Ye wives, how do you know when you love your husbands? Ye parents, how do you know when you love your children?'" He had concluded by saying that they would be bound to reply, "'I feel it.'" That was also how they could know that they loved God.[51] Another Methodist heard much the same sermon at the society-room in London, but on that occasion anyway found Wesley unpersuasive. In a letter to Charles she wrote that Wesley had "put it very close to us whether we did Love God." Then, she said, he had continued, "'Some of you will say, how shall we know if we love God?'" Perhaps this time Wesley was straining too hard to make his point. For when he followed through with his rhetorical comparison—"'it was as easie to know as to know whether we was hot or cold'"—his hearer noted, "I thought it was not."[52]

Along with his preaching about the love of God, he also gave the flock explicit warnings against "Idolatrous Love" for him. He gave these warnings "often," and they were needed. For as one Methodist confessed, she had for about a year "rather esteem'd him as a Savior than a Minister." In that "Dreadful State" she had never been at rest except when she was "with him or hearing him talked of."[53] Nor was this frame of mind confined to women. Men might feel the same for him, might also put him in the place of God. This was probably what had happened to the Cornishman who said just before dying, "I shall soon see the smiling face of Wesley."[54]

[50]David D. Hall, *The Faithful Shepherd* (Chapel Hill, N.C., 1972), p. 17.
[51]James Barrit autobiography, Methodist Archive.
[52]Joan Webb to Charles Wesley, May 1742, ibid.
[53]Elizabeth Halfpenny to Charles Wesley, May 1742, ibid.
[54]Thomas Shaw, *A History of Cornish Methodism* (Truro, 1967), p. 76.

John Greenwood after N. Hone, *John Wesley, M.A. Fellow of Lincoln College, Oxford*, 1770, mezzotint (Olin Library Collection, Wesleyan University, Middletown, Connecticut).

James Philip de Loutherbourg, "A Midsummer Afternoon with a Methodist Preacher," 1777, oil on canvas (National Gallery of Canada, Ottawa).

A. Biggerman, *The Death of the Revd. John Wesley, A.M., c. 1860,* lithograph with hand-coloring (Davison Art Center Collection, Wesleyan University, Middletown, Connecticut).

In fact whole communities might share the infatuation. At Athlone, for instance, he preached in 1748 to an adoring crowd, and when he had finished the sermon and started to ride away, about a hundred of his listeners followed, unwilling to part with him. A mile along the way he stopped to sing a last hymn with them, and they cried. Drafting his Journal entry for the day, he commented, "If the people of Athlone did but love God as they do me, they would be the praise of the whole earth." On rereading the draft, he decided to keep that comment to himself. It touched a tender spot. He edited it out of the text of the Journal as published.[55]

Edit as he would, the worry that he was monopolizing his followers' love remained. When finally he lay dying, after fifty-one years as a traveling evangelist, the worry may possibly have intensified. For his last request, according to Elizabeth Ritchie, the Yorkshire Methodist who nursed him, was that some sermon of his on "the love of God" be printed and distributed without charge, to "everybody." To communicate this request to those around him, debilitated as he then was, Wesley had to make a "great exertion." Even so his words could hardly be distinguished.[56] During the course of the next morning, he died.

Before the burial, Wesley's request was complied with. Ten thousand copies of a nearly appropriate sermon were printed and given away free.[57] Meantime Miss Ritchie contrived to cut off a lock of his hair to keep as a memento.[58]

[55]Curnock, 3: 345.

[56]For Miss Ritchie's report, see Curnock, 8: 139. One other witness of Wesley's last request left a report of it, too. This was the helper, James Rogers. What Rogers said corresponds exactly to what Miss Ritchie said: Wesley asked that a sermon of his on the "LOVE OF GOD" be given to "every one." James Rogers, *The Experience and Labours of James Rogers, Preacher of the Gospel* (Bristol, 1796), p. 48.

[57]His colleagues chose and printed *God's Love to Fallen Man: A Sermon on Romans V. 15* (London, 1791). It was nearly but not quite appropriate. Wesley had specified a sermon on "the love of God." Both of the two extant reports of his words agree on that. But they chose a sermon on "God's love." It may be that their choice shows them defending, in the psychoanalytical sense of the word, against a full realization of what Wesley was finally saying.

[58]*The Homes, Haunts, and Friends of John Wesley: Being the Centenary Number of the Methodist Recorder* (rev. and enlarged ed.; London, 1891), p. 2.

Chapter Four

The Limits of Wesley's Influence

Wesley had started his evangelical traveling in the late 1730's, at a time when revivalist sentiment was sweeping virtually the whole Protestant world. In the North American colonies, in Scotland, in Germany, many preachers were traveling and drawing crowds and making converts; and even in England, Wesley was only one among scores, or maybe hundreds, who were telling in the highways "the glad tidings of salvation." But the movement that Wesley headed turned out differently from the other revivals. It lasted and grew steadily bigger, while the rest either petered out entirely or became weaker and less stable as time passed.

These differences may now perhaps be explained. Wesley in his self-presentation played the gentleman with resourcefulness and verve, using every traditional counter he could, and he exacted deference. Such other gentlemen as he came across, he regarded as rivals or obstacles, hardly as subjects in their own right. Even his colleagues he treated as rivals, and he kept them down. Wesley also won and monopolized love. He eclipsed his colleagues and even God Almighty in the hearts of his followers. Their deference might be impermanent, and their enthusiasm might decline in a naturally developing ebb of feeling, but their love kept them fixed in place. Wesley's accomplishment was unique. No other contemporary revivalist managed a pastoral stance so strangely monopolistic and seductive; no other achieved a comparable result.

To give immediacy to this contrast between Wesley and his revivalist contemporaries, think for a moment of two tableaux. Think first of Wesley as he was, say, at Athlone on the day he wrote in his Journal the comment that he later refrained from publishing, that if the Athloners loved God as well as they loved him, they would be the praise of the whole earth. That was the time a crowd followed him a mile along the way as he rode out of town and then cried when he stopped to sing a last hymn with them. Or think of him, say, two years later at Athlone, when again he had finished meeting with the congregation and "would have dismissed them," but "none seemed willing to go." So they remained, he in his ensemble, they as they were, just "standing and looking at each other."[1]

Next, another tableau: think of Jonathan Edwards as he typically appeared to his flock at Northampton. Edwards may be especially suitable for comparison to Wesley. The two men were exact contemporaries, both born in 1703. Besides, they were true peers, both university-trained, both ordained, both devout, both evangelical. Of the many preachers who rode the revivalist wave that started to crest in the late 1730's, they were also probably the two ablest intellectually. Moreover, each admired the work of the other, so far as he knew it. Wesley published British editions of two of Edwards's revivalist tracts, and in a gesture of homage and compliment that he never repeated for any other author, sent copies of both to every bishop of the Church of England.[2] Edwards probably knew less of Wesley than Wesley knew of him. He had never spent time in England as Wesley had in America, and the British correspondents to whom Edwards wrote were mostly Scottish. Still, he was enormously impressed by what he heard of the first years of the revival in England.[3]

[1]Nehemiah Curnock, ed., *The Journal of the Rev. John Wesley, A.M.* (London, 1909–16), 3: 345, 483.

[2]This gesture was recorded in John Bennet's minutes of the conference between Wesley and his helpers and clerical sympathizers held in 1744. *Proceedings of the Wesley Historical Society*, 1 (1898): 30. The tracts Wesley sent to the bishops were *The Distinguishing Marks of a Work of the Spirit of God* and *A Faithful Narrative of the Surprizing Work of God*. He had edited out everything in them that conflicted with his own stand on free grace.

[3]See Henry Abelove, "Jonathan Edwards's Letter of Invitation to George Whitefield," *William and Mary Quarterly*, 24 (July 1972): 488–89. For more on transatlantic communication among the eighteenth-century revivalists, see Susan O'Brien, "A Transatlantic Community of Saints," *American Historical Review*, 91 (Oct. 1986): 811–32.

Edwards often spent his afternoons walking and meditating in the woods around Northampton. He would carry pins and paper with him, and when he got an idea he would note it on a bit of paper and pin the paper to his coat, or sometimes he would leave the paper blank and pin it to his coat just as a mnemonic device. By the time he headed back to town in the late afternoon and returned to public view after his walk and meditation were done, his coat would be covered with pinned-on bits of paper. So unconcerned was he with exacting deference that he would let his townspeople see him literally wearing the signs of his insufficiency.[4] They would see him also, and maybe more commonly, in the pulpit. Edwards preached well, thoughtfully, and affectingly, but as he preached he usually looked upward, avoiding the eyes and faces of the congregation, eschewing any sort of seductiveness. It seemed to them as though he were staring at the bellrope, which descended inside the meeting house from the belfry to the front gallery. "He looked on the bellrope," one observer remarked, "until he looked it off."[5] His strained angle of vision, so rigidly unalluring, even came to be something of a joke in town, especially after the time one Sunday when the rope snapped. It was "cut asunder" by his eyes, the local jokers said.[6]

Doubtless Wesley suffered in consequence of the love he won from his followers, worried that he was monopolizing it, deflecting it from God, felt guilty and anxious. But he never experienced a loss like the one Edwards did. Edwards saw the revival that he had so carefully nourished and so greatly valued decline to nothing in a few years' time. It had rippled in 1734, got fully under way in 1740, and was finished by 1742, or 1744 at the latest. Some years after that his townspeople, who had after all never been made to love him, took his pulpit away too. He then had to leave town and accept a post in the wilderness.[7] Wesley, who had bound his followers to himself by both def-

[4]Perry Miller, *Jonathan Edwards* (New York, 1949), p. 50. See also William E. Park, "The Edwardean: Notes for a Biography of Jonathan Edwards," Beinecke Library, Yale University, New Haven, Conn.

[5]Quoted by Miller, p. 51.

[6]Park, "Edwardean."

[7]I do not mean to imply that Edwards was never loved. Since the eighteenth century some readers have been attracted to him on account of his intellectual power, his sparse sensibility, and his many losses. Robert Lowell was one of them, and he wrote of Edwards: "I love you faded, / old, exiled and afraid / to leave your last flock,

erence and love, presided over a revival that so long as he lived never intermitted or declined.

Wesley knew the difference, of course, between the outcome of his revival and that of the others that had begun at about the same time. In 1755 he made that difference the subject of a sermon, which he delivered to the Methodists of London. As his text he chose Psalms 147 : 20: God "hath not dealt so with any nation." As his application he explained triumphantly, "no, not even with Scotland or New England." God, Wesley went on to say, had certainly "wrought" in Scotland and New England, and "at several times," but each time just "for some weeks or months together, without any observable intermission."[8] All the revivalists kept themselves informed as best they could concerning the spiritual news from foreign parts, and the information about the course of the revival in Scotland and New England, which Wesley gave in the course of this sermon, was entirely accurate. Had he wished to particularize further concerning the American scene, he could have added that as of the moment he was speaking, Edwards had already spent about four years as an exile in the wilderness.

Was Wesley conscious of what he was doing in his relationship with his flock? Did he intend by exacting deference and winning love to hold them to himself so that his revival might be uniquely continuous? One way of answering might be to say that even those whose mode of self-presentation is the most calculated of all, even actors, cannot usually explain just how they get the effects they get. That is the job of the critic, who can compare their performance with that of others, who can watch them again and again, maybe on slow-motion film, and who in any case knows how to explain. Explaining is the critic's specialty, just as art is the actor's. It is by no means necessary to believe that Wesley could have said in detail just how he

---

a dozen / Housatonic Indian children." Lowell, *For the Union Dead* (New York, 1965), p. 43. Edwards's career eventually reblossomed. But at the time he had to leave Northampton, and for some of the time he spent in Stockbridge, he felt like an exile.

[8] I quote from the summary of the sermon that Wesley printed in his Journal. Curnock, 4: 122. Wesley accounted for the relative failure of the other revivals in his characteristic way: they had lapsed because their leaders had fallen into the sins of "pride, bitterness, bigotry" and "self-indulgence." Ibid., p. 123. He was always a hard rival.

made the impact that he made. To say that must be the job of the historian, who stands to Wesley in much the same relation as the critic does to the actor. The historian also can make relevant comparisons, can think through the past record again and again, and presumably can explain.

But even if Wesley could not have said in detail just how he made the impact that he made, he certainly was conscious in a general way of what he was doing. He knew that he managed by exacting deference. That was why he could understand Charles's warning that a marriage to Grace Murray would have wrecked "ye work of God," why he could respond to the warning with a rationale for his behavior designed to satisfy nineteen in twenty of the helpers and societies. He knew that he managed also by winning love. That was why he worried that some of his flock preferred him to God. He knew, too, that he was succeeding in making his revival last. That was why he could contrast it with the short-lived revivals in North America and Scotland.

In short, Wesley understood what he was achieving, and he achieved it by the means that his master had long before promised, or warned, would work: "For the kingdom of heaven suffereth violence, and the violent bear it away."[9]

Wesley bore it away. In 1767 the full-fledged members of the Methodist societies in the British Isles numbered 25,911; in 1777, 38,274; in 1787, 62,088; and by the time Wesley died in 1791, 72,476.[10] In addition, there were thousands of people who never formally joined a society but were still Methodists, still followers of Wesley.[11]

[9]Matt. 11 : 12.

[10]*Minutes of the Methodist Conferences* (London, 1862), 1: 72, 130, 201, 252.

[11]Since the 1970's there has been a small surge of good scholarship on the demography of Methodism. See, for instance, Alan D. Gilbert, *Religion and Society in Industrial England* (London, 1976), pp. 30–31. But this scholarship attends almost only to the full-fledged, ticket-carrying Methodists. This is anachronistic. It is to treat the Methodism of Wesley's day as though it were the same as the closed-in, sectarian Methodism of the nineteenth century. But the Methodism of Wesley's day was not a sect. It was a revival, a field of force. It kept many adherents and affected many others without involving them in formal membership. As Wesley once remarked, "I see plainly we have often judged amiss when we have measured the increase of the work of God, in this and other places, by the increase of the society

It might be supposed that because Wesley had magnetized all these many thousands, because they deferred to him and loved him, they would do anything he asked, learn what he taught, believe what he said. But that supposition would be mistaken. For the result of their attachment to him was not just docility. It was something else as well, something almost contrary to docility. It was union with one another.[12]

Wesley observed this himself as he traveled. At Sheerness he found that the flock were "of one heart and one mind"; at Burslem, "much united in affection"; at Worcester, "lovingly and closely knit together"; at Bristol, "united" like "a family of love." At Plymouth Dock he said that they "cleave close together," and at Macclesfield, much moved by their union, he exclaimed, "Here was the harmony which art cannot imitate."[13]

What Wesley observed of them, they also observed of themselves. "Our hearts," a Gloucestershire man said, speaking of his fellow Methodists and of himself, were "so knot together, that each could have put ye other in his bosom."[14] Sometimes this sense of union led spontaneously to song, as for instance among the Methodists of Horbury, who used to sing as they walked together in the evening through the woods the several miles they had to go to get to the preaching:

> Break forth into singing ye trees of the wood;
> For Jesus is bringing lost sinners to God[15]

---

only." Curnock, 3: 360. For the demographers, of course, the problem is that adherents cannot easily be made into statistics, while full-fledged members can. For a rationale and defense of the demographers' reliance on membership rolls, see Robert Currie, Alan Gilbert, and Lee Horsley, *Churches and Churchgoers* (Oxford, 1977), pp. 14–20.

[12]In my view, Freud provides a persuasive answer to the question of why they should have felt so united, after having first felt attracted to Wesley: when a group of people put "one and the same object in the place of their ego ideal," they then identify themselves "with one another in their ego." Sigmund Freud, *Group Psychology and the Analysis of the Ego*, vol. 18 of James Strachey et al., eds., *The Standard Edition of the Complete Psychological Works of Sigmund Freud* (London, 1955), p. 116. Moreover, Freud suggests that the "object" may sometimes be an idea rather than a person; ibid., p. 100.

[13]Curnock, 7: 213, 371; 5: 355; 6: 397; 7: 244; 6: 346.

[14]William Holder diary, Oct. 14, 1768, Methodist Archive.

[15]Thomas Jackson, ed., *The Lives of the Early Methodist Preachers, Chiefly Written by Themselves* (London, 1838), 3: 276.

Another group of Methodists, returning from a sermon, rode through Bandon one night, and as they rode they "all joined heartily" in a hymn, "to the no small surprize of the inhabitants, who came out of their houses and looked . . . with astonishment."[16] Similarly at Peel the local flock lined the highway one night, waiting for the arrival of one of the helpers, to guide him through the "dark," and when he arrived, led him into town, "rejoicing and singing" together all the way.[17]

Because of their union, so warm that it led even to spontaneous song, the Methodists as a group were often attractive to those around them, particularly to the lonely and the desperate. Take the case of a certain non-Methodist, a Shetland Islander who was driven by need from his home and family at Lerwick in 1772 and had to set off for England in search of work. He took with him just eight and a half shillings in cash and a small batch of Shetland stockings worth three pounds that he meant to sell as the need arose. When he reached Dundee he arranged for passage on a sloop bound for Newcastle, but unfavorable winds delayed the ship's departure. During the delay he boarded with a family and paid onepence a night for bed. He ate as sparely as he could so as to conserve his small capital, and on Sundays he went to church. One Sunday he stopped at the "Methodists meeting" and found that he could get no farther than the doorway because "they were so throng" there. Eventually the sloop sailed, and he got to Newcastle. From there he went to Sunderland, then to Portsmouth, and finally to London, where he felt himself "like a blind man without a guide." He had less money than when he had started, his batch of stockings was depleted, he had no notion where to go to find work, and he was "friendless." He ate even more sparely than before, applied for jobs but got nothing, walked the streets, and passed the Bank of England, where he "seed the Gold lying in heaps." His first and only Saturday night in London, he spent at his inn, "very solitarry" and "supping on bread and cheese as usual." On Sunday he did not go to church but did go "to the Methodists meeting." After the sermon he returned to the inn, again "solitarry" in his room, and wrote these verses:

[16]Richard Burdsall, *Memoirs of the Life of Richard Burdsall* (3d ed.; Thetford, 1823), p. 139.
[17]John Crook diary, Nov. 10, 1775, Methodist Archive.

Now at London in a garret room I am,
here friendless and forsaken;
But from the Lord my help will come,
Who trusts in him are not mistaken.

When friends on earth do faint and faile,
And upon you their backs do turn;
O Truely seek the Lord, and he will
Them comfort that do murn.

I'll unto God my prayer make,
to him my case make known;
And hopes he will for Jesus sake,
Provide for me and soon.

But no work turned up the next day, or the next. "Hundreds," he noted, "were starving for want of employment," and on Wednesday, when he was down to his last shilling, he sold himself as an indentured servant bound for Virginia. He never saw his wife or children again and died in Virginia two years later. While he teetered on the edge of the decision to sell himself, with nobody to turn to, the "throng" at the Methodist preaching-houses—the crowd, the warmth—attracted him, as they attracted many others, in a similarly desperate condition.[18]

"Throng" though they were, the Methodists' union with one another was never free of strain. Disagreements arose and sometimes festered. Their letters and conversation were filled with sad reports of "disputes and animosities" and of "many little differences."[19] Because the society was so close the differences were a matter of grave concern, and the Methodists often had to pray for an end to strain. If the strain continued nonetheless, they tried to comfort each other as best they could. As one man told his fellow Methodists, the "closest joints" in a building were produced by "the rubbing of stones one against another." Similarly, he said consolingly, their quarrels, their "rubs one against another," would inevitably make their "union the closer."[20]

[18]Edward Miles Riley, ed., *The Journal of John Harrower* (Williamsburg, Va., 1963), especially pp. 5, 14–17.
[19]Mary Ramsey to Charles Wesley, June 4, 1740, Methodist Archive; Robert Dickinson, *Life of the Rev. John Braithwaite* (London, 1825), p. 39.
[20]Burdsall, 270.

Despite their "rubs," or perhaps as this consoler suggested, on account of them, the Methodists' sense of solidarity remained strong. One of the consequences of this closing of ranks was that they organized. It is sometimes said that Wesley was an especially good organizer. That is mistaken. He was not. The Methodists organized themselves entirely on their own initiative. Wesley was the center of their union. So long as he was there they could feel their ties to one another and act mutually. But they made the organization. All three of the great organizational features of Methodism were popular initiatives: the acquisition of preaching-houses, the use of lay preaching, and the device of the class meeting. Of these three the first two Wesley even initially opposed.[21]

United, organized, they were by no means just passive receivers of his teaching. Their attachment to him was real and deep, but so was their attachment to one another. They heard what he said, but they heard it in ways that suited themselves mutually. As a result the Methodism they lived out was different from anything that he taught. It was a compromise between his word and their need.

But what was his word, anyway? What did Wesley try to teach them? And what did they actually learn? These questions are now appropriate and may best be considered under three successive headings: sexuality, spirituality, and daily conduct.

[21]Wesley was persuaded to lease the first Methodist preaching-house, the London Foundery. He felt reluctant to do so. Luke Tyerman, *The Life and Times of the Rev. John Wesley, A.M.* (2d ed; London, 1870–72), 1: 271. He was also persuaded against his own initial inclination to take on the first helper. Frank Baker, "The People Called Methodists—3. Polity," in Rupert Davies and Gordon Rupp, eds., *A History of the Methodist Church in Great Britain* (London, 1965), 1: 230. Here the persuader may have been his mother, who was by then a member of his flock. The third of the great organizational features of Methodism, the class meeting, was suggested by a member of the Bristol flock in 1742. This suggestion Wesley readily accepted. Baker, "People Called Methodists," p. 222.

Chapter Five

Sexuality

Wesley wanted the Methodists who were converted to refrain if they could from marrying, and he told them so repeatedly, both in print and in exhortation. He first published his views on the subject in 1743, early in his career, in the pamphlet *Thoughts on Marriage and a Single Life*. Here he said that he had often been asked which was to be "preferr'd," a "Married State, or a Single Life," and that he had decided to write out an answer. It was that the "Single Life" was better, at least for believers, and in fact was required of them.[1]

This answer Wesley grounded on Scripture, particularly on the passage in the Gospel of Matthew where Jesus says: "And there be eunuchs which have made themselves eunuchs for the kingdom of heaven's sake. He that is able to receive it, let him receive it." Wesley thought that the meaning of the passage was clear: that "eunuchs which have made themselves eunuchs" meant persons who "have abstain'd from Marriage all their Lives, have remain'd Single 'till Death"; that "he who is able to receive it" meant "Every believer in Christ"; and that "let him receive it" was a plain order, a command.[2] So the passage was to be understood as commanding that every believer stay single and celibate.

Wesley acknowledged that his reading of the passage was more rigorous even than that of the "Romish writers." They said that Jesus

---

[1]John Wesley, *Thoughts on Marriage and a Single Life* (Bristol, 1743), pp. 2, 10. I quote from the printing designated as 1b in Frank Baker, *Union Catalogue of the Publications of John and Charles Wesley* (Durham, N.C., 1966), p. 47.

[2]Ibid., pp. 6–9, expounding Matt. 19 : 12.

was not commanding celibacy there but rather counseling it, and that although everybody was supposed to keep his commands, his counsels were not obligatory. But according to Wesley, nothing in the text justified a distinction between counsels and commands. Such a distinction had "no place" anywhere in Scripture, least of all in that particular passage in Matthew. After all, the words were not, "He may receive it, if he will," but, "Let him receive it." These words were certainly a command. "How," Wesley asked, "could a Command be more clearly exprest?"[3]

It was a command addressed, moreover, to all converts, or as they were also called, justified persons. For they were the ones "able to receive it," the ones who had the gift of continence. That gift they had got at the time of their "Redemption." At that moment, "lust" had vanished, and so long as they kept themselves in the faith, praying and looking to Jesus day and night, lust would "never return."[4]

But what if converts were already married, already "bound," at the time of their "Redemption"? In that case they should continue to be married, continue willingly to satisfy the sexual wants of their partners. "Support" would come to them "therein" from God. All other converts should be eunuchs for the sake of heaven. It was at once their privilege and their duty. If, however, they faltered in faith, if they were insufficiently watchful and prayerful, then they might lose the gift of continence and become "weak again," like ordinary people. In that situation they should marry, unless they felt very sure that they could recover the lost gift "soon." For without that gift they might easily slide into the sin of fornication, and marriage was of course preferable to fornication.[5]

Wesley also warned that nobody should forbid marriage or despise it or foster divorce.[6] Still, he made clear that marriage was second-best. Celibacy was what Jesus wanted, and he wanted it of all those who were born again, so long as they stayed faithful and did not happen to be married already.

This view was not unique to Wesley. There were at least two other revivalists during the great mid-eighteenth-century revival who put

[3]Ibid., pp. 6–7.
[4]Ibid., p. 9.
[5]Ibid., pp. 9–11.
[6]Ibid., pp. 3–5.

a comparably high value on lay celibacy, both obscure, both based in the North American colonies—Shadrach Ireland, who led a small sect in Harvard, Massachusetts, and Johann Konrad Beissel, who founded a quasi-monastic community at Ephrata, Pennsylvania— and during the first Christian centuries, a commitment to sexual renunciation was common among the adherents of the new faith.[7] So Wesley's view was not unheard-of. Still, it was highly unusual, at least in Protestant tradition, and was not shared by his helpers and sympathizers. In fact they opposed his view, and forcefully enough to persuade him to modify it a little.[8] When he published a second time on the same subject, in 1765, his argument showed some signs of their influence.

He called his new pamphlet *Thoughts on a Single Life*, and here he again maintained that the single life was preferable for the converted. But he no longer said, as he had before, that it was required of them. He also acknowledged that the gift of continence, which every justified person got at the time of his conversion, did not "continue long" with most. It was in fact usually withdrawn, perhaps on account of some "Fault" in the convert. Then marriage was called for, and Wesley said something about it especially positive. In the previous pamphlet he had said that nobody should forbid it or despise

---

[7]C. C. Goen, *Revivalism and Separatism in New England* (New Haven, Conn., 1962), p. 201; Julius Friedrich Sachse, *The German Sectarians of Pennsylvania, 1708–1742* (Philadelphia, 1899), 1: 254–56. Most Protestants have been opposed even to clerical celibacy. See Steven Ozment, "Marriage and Ministry in the Protestant Churches," in William Bassett and Peter Huizing, eds., *Celibacy in the Church* (New York, 1972), pp. 39–56. On sexual renunciation in early Christianity, see Peter Brown, *The Body and Society* (New York, 1988).

[8]See J. A. Leger, *John Wesley's Last Love* (London, 1910), p. 1. Wesley explained that he had modified his view after a "full and friendly debate" with his colleagues in 1748. They disliked his view then, and their successors have continued to dislike it since, so much so that they have taken to omitting any discussion of it from their histories of Methodism. One of the last of the Methodist preachers to give space in a history book to Wesley's extraordinary view on marriage was Luke Tyerman, and his comment was, "What shall we say of this?" *The Life and Times of the Rev. John Wesley, A.M.* (London, 1870–72), 1: 432. In 1909 Herbert Workman alluded to it by comparing Methodism to monasticism. W. J. Townsend, H. B. Workman, and George Eayrs, eds., *A New History of Methodism* (London, 1909), 1: 41. As a result of this denominational reticence, which has all but buried the pertinent sources, no historian of sex till now has noticed just how extreme Wesley's position actually was.

it. Now he went a step further and said that "persons may be as holy in a married as it is possible to be in a single State."[9]

That was certainly a concession to his colleagues, and almost as though to counterbalance it, he included a fervent listing of the advantages enjoyed exclusively by those who stayed single. They alone could serve God without distraction, for they were "exempt" from "the numberless Occasions of Sorrow and Anxiety with which Heads of Families are intangled: Especially those, who have sickly or weak, or unhappy, or disobedient children." Servants, Wesley explained, could be fired if they proved unsatisfactory. But children, even when bad or unhealthy, remained as a permanent encumbrance to their parents. This encumbrance single people escaped.[10]

Another advantage was that they were safe from "the greatest of all Intanglements, the loving One Creature above all others." It was possible, Wesley said, to love a spouse without sin. Possible, yes: "But how inconceivably difficult." Sexual intercourse would always be a snare. Lovers could hardly tell how to gratify their desire just so far as "Christian Temperance" allowed, and no further.[11] Yet another advantage that single people enjoyed was leisure. While married people were necessarily busied with "the things of the world," single people were free to improve themselves in the spirit, to wait on God continuously, and were free also to do good to their neighbors, so far at least as "Christian Prudence" might allow. They need ask nobody's permission; they could freely take the time to do as they thought best.[12]

Finally, single people need accumulate no wealth. They could give all their earnings to God. A married man would have a wife and perhaps also children "to provide for," and he would probably wonder doubtfully and anxiously how far he was right in accumulating for their sake, whether he was doing "too much or too little for them." From all such doubts and anxieties, single people were entirely free. They had nobody to consider except God.[13]

Having listed these advantages, Wesley went on to urge that single

---

[9] John Wesley, *Thoughts on a Single Life* (London, 1765), pp. 3–5. I quote from the printing that Baker, *Union Catalogue*, p. 122, lists first.

[10] Ibid., p. 5.

[11] Ibid., pp. 5–6.

[12] Ibid., p. 6.

[13] Ibid.

people "prize" them and "keep" them and "use" them. He also gave a few prudential warnings. Single people who were trying to hold onto the gift of continence they had got at their conversion would be well advised to converse often with "like-minded" persons of their own sex and to avoid "all needless Conversation, much more all Intimacy," with "those of the Other Sex." They should also refrain from masturbating ("Satan will not cast out Satan," Wesley explained), and they should live hard, eschewing "self-indulgence" and "delicacy" and "softness," exercising as much as their strength allowed and spending as little time in bed as possible.[14]

Wesley expressed his preference for celibacy not only in these pamphlets but also in his pastoral conduct and arrangements. First of all, he exhorted. He told the unmarried to stay as they were. Especially in the bigger societies, where there were sizable groups of young, still single people, Wesley would from time to time meet with them, men and women separately, and encourage them, tell them how "good" it was to remain single, urge them "to consider, to prize, and to improve" their advantages.[15]

Along with his exhortations he would repeat the warning against masturbation that he had given in the second of his celibacy pamphlets. He would also doctor those he thought were suffering from the ill-effects of masturbation. For Wesley shared the view common among physicians of his day that persistent masturbating was bound to lead to illness and possibly to death. Typical symptoms might be paleness, effeminacy, loss of appetite, weakened eyesight, paralysis, convulsions, or "the most painful of all gouts."[16] In treating the symptoms Wesley followed the guidance of the Swiss physician Samuel Tissot, whose book on the subject he pirated, abridged, and in part rewrote for the use of the flock.[17] Chiefly, Wesley advised the sufferer

[14]Ibid., pp. 7–9.

[15]Nehemiah Curnock, ed., *The Journal of the Rev. John Wesley, A.M.* (London, 1909–16), 3: 512; 7: 51. See also *Memoirs of James Lackington, Written by Himself* (New York, 1796), p. 10.

[16][John Wesley], *Thoughts on the Sin of Onan, Chiefly Extracted from a Late Writer* (London, 1767), p. 4. I quote from the printing that Baker, *Union Catalogue*, p. 130, lists first.

[17]Samuel Tissot, *Onanism; or a Treatise Upon the Disorders Produced by Masturbation*, tr. A. Hume (London, 1766). On Tissot, see the essay by Ludmilla Jordanova, "The Popularization of Medicine," *Textual Practice*, 1 (1987): 68–80. For a general

to breathe the morning air and to drink milk. He noted that the milk of the human female was "generally believed to be the most strengthening" kind, but that it had to be sucked direct from the breast, and this made for a difficulty. If the sufferer sucked at the breast direct, he might feel a "temptation." In most cases cow's milk would be good enough.[18]

Wesley also tried to guard the Methodists from those evangelical Christians who took a comparatively positive view of sex. Here the worst offenders were the Moravians, the German pietists who had been instrumental in leading Wesley himself to conversion. Nearly all his evangelical contemporaries were warmer toward marriage than he was; but the Moravians were downright pro-sex, or so at least Wesley thought, and this attitude of theirs was one of the several causes for his early break with them. He quoted Count Nicolaus Zinzendorf, the leader of the Moravians, as having said that Jesus had been incarnated a man, so that the "Male Member" might be sanctified, and born of a woman, so that the female genitals might be made equally "honourable." Zinzendorf's effort to give a positive religious sanction to human sex was horrible to Wesley, and he wanted it to be equally so to his flock. "Were ever such words put together before," he asked, referring indignantly to these and other similar comments by Zinzendorf, "from the Foundation of the World?"[19]

Wesley even opposed the institution of the family pew, something that was then usual both in the churches of the Establishment and in the chapels of Dissent. No doubt he disliked the ostentation that often went along with these pews. In many chapels they were virtually closed-off rooms, resembling parlors, lined with baize and covered by curtains.[20] No doubt he disliked also the institution of reserved seats. He wanted the Methodist preaching-houses to be open

---

account of the fear of masturbation in European history, see Jean Stengers and Anne Van Neck, *Histoire d'une grande peur* (Brussels, 1984).

[18][Wesley], *Thoughts on the Sins of Onan*, pp. 13–16. In his comments on women's milk, Wesley was largely following Tissot, pp. 98–99. Both believed that the milk replaced the lost genital fluid of the masturbator.

[19] John Wesley, *Queries Proposed to the Right Reverend and Right Honourable Count Zinzendorf* (London, 1755), pp. 27–28. I quote from the printing that Baker, *Union Catalogue*, p. 99, lists first.

[20] B. L. Manning, "Some Characteristics of the Older Dissent," *Congregational Quarterly*, 5 (July 1927): 292.

to anybody who might want to enter them. But Wesley's chief objection was neither to ostentation nor to reserved seating, for he did not willingly permit family pews that were unostentatious, nor did he want families to sit together even on seats that were unreserved. His chief objection was to the mixing of the sexes. He ordered that the seating for worship in the Methodist preaching-houses be entirely segregated by sex, with a rail set between the women and the men.[21]

Wesley also tried to arrange for Methodist fellowship meetings to be segregated by sex. From the very start of his career as a traveling evangelist, he divided the flock who were already converted into bands. These were small groups, whose members met regularly for mutual edification and guidance. At the meetings each person present would be asked:

1. What known sin have you committed since our last meeting?
2. What temptations have you met with?
3. How were you delivered?
4. What have you thought, said, or done, of which you doubt whether it be a sin or not?
5. Have you nothing you desire to keep secret?[22]

Naturally these questions and their answers produced a kind of intimacy, and because the bands were constituted as all male or all female, the intimacy was kept guardedly intrasexual. Alongside the bands Wesley established another sort of group for fellowship, the select-bands. These were smaller and fewer than the bands and included just the Methodists who were already Perfected, or who were pressing on to Perfection. Here the purposes of meeting were also mutual edification and guidance, and the intimacy was more intense

[21]John Telford, ed., *The Letters of the Rev. John Wesley, A.M.* (London, 1931), 7: 215. Separate seating by sex was not of course a new usage. It had been common in the primitive church, it was practiced by the Quakers, and the First Book of Common Prayer had required it at communion. See James White, *Protestant Worship and Church Architecture* (Oxford, 1964).

[22]Quoted by Frank Baker, "The People Called Methodists—3. Polity," in Rupert Davies and Gordon Rupp, eds., *A History of the Methodist Church in Great Britain* (London, 1965), 1: 219. Eventually the fifth queston was dropped. Wesley developed his band system with the Moravian choirs in mind. On the choirs, see Gillian Gollin, *Moravians in Two Worlds* (New York, 1967), pp. 67–89.

even than in the bands. For there was a special rule that nothing said in select-band could ever be repeated to anybody else. These groups as well were segregated by sex.[23]

Finally, Wesley made his preference for celibacy perfectly clear by his attitude toward marriage ceremonies. He disliked the work of performing them, and he chose to perform very few. In his Journal he recorded still fewer. From his conversion in 1738 until his death in 1791, throughout the whole length of his career as a traveling evangelist, he mentioned in the Journal only four marriages that he had officiated at or assisted at. Of these four, one was a family affair that he could hardly have escaped, the marriage of his brother Charles. During that same period, by contrast, he mentioned 104 funerals that he had officiated at or assisted at or preached at.[24] Funerals, Wesley believed, might edify; marriages were best avoided. His reluctance to perform marriages may even have been one of the private motives behind his public decision to make his career as an itinerant rather than as a parish clergyman. If he had taken a parish in the usual way, he would have been canonically obliged to perform marriages—lots of them.

But how did Wesley square the facts of his own family life with his commitment to celibacy? After all, he tried to marry one woman, Grace Murray, and actually married another, Mrs. Vazeille. Besides, he was the son of a married couple whose Christian practice he often spoke of as exemplary.

Wesley never got the opportunity to explain to his flock why he was entitled to Grace Murray. She was taken away from him too quickly, and for reasons entirely untheological. His fellow Methodists believed that if he were to marry a woman like her, of plebeian origins, he would make a disgraceful misalliance that could put the success of the whole Methodist movement at risk. They took her away from him fast and jockeyed her into marriage with somebody else. But in the memoir he wrote about his relationship with her, there are some clear hints of how he would have made the case for

---

[23] Baker, "Polity," p. 225.

[24] For a full list of these marriages and funerals, see Henry Abelove, "John Wesley's Influence During His Lifetime on the Methodists" (Ph.D. dissertation, Yale University, 1978), pp. 221–30.

his marrying her, had he got the opportunity. First he would have said that his colleagues had lately convinced him that married people could live as holy as single people.[25] That would have been true, of course. Still, to have said just that and no more would have been to give a minimal excuse for the marriage, and Wesley meant to go further. He would have said also that Grace Murray was of unique value to him in his work as a traveling evangelist, that she was "undeniably" the "most usefull woman in ye Kingdom." He would have demanded of his flock that they "shew me ye Woman in England, Wales, or Ireland, who has already done so much Good as G. M." Then he would have demanded: "Shew me one in all ye English Annals, whom God has employ'd in so high a degree. I might say, In all ye History of the Church, from ye Death of our Lord to this day."[26] To these demands the flock could presumably have replied nothing. So extraordinary a vessel as that would have only too obviously been due the leader of the movement, regardless of ordinary rules. Finally, Wesley might have been willing, if necessary, to say that he had lost the gift of continence and felt obliged to marry.[27]

How he explained his right to Mrs. Vazeille, the woman whom he did marry, I have already described. He said that only by marrying could he protect himself and the good reputation of the movement from scandalmongers, from people like the Bishop of Exeter, who accused him of libertinism just because he was unmarried. About two weeks before the ceremony he met with the single men of the London society and urged them to stay single. That was what was best, he explained, "unless," adding a qualification meant to cover his own plans, "where a particular case might be an exception to the general rule."[28]

As for his parents, Wesley hardly acknowledged their marriage, and all but claimed for himself a virgin birth. His father died in 1735 before the Methodist flock was yet in existence; his mother lived longer, into the 1740's, and when she died Wesley had already become the successful head of a growing movement. In his mourning he sent

[25]Leger, p. 1.
[26]Ibid., p. 73.
[27]Ibid., p. 74.
[28]Curnock, 3:512.

every member of the London bands an engraved portrait of his mother and made the funeral a public occasion.[29] A big crowd of Methodists attended, Wesley read the service and then committed her body to the earth, "to sleep," he wrote in his Journal, "with her fathers."[30] He made no mention of her husband, and he persisted in this omission even in the inscription he later put on her tombstone. In an extraordinary break with convention, he described her there, on the stone, as "Mrs. Susannah Wesley, the Youngest and Last Surviving Daughter of Dr. Samuel Annesley," with no hint that she had ever been married.[31] Wesley held that back—or rather, he nearly held it back. For he did not succeed in holding it back altogether. When he bought the burial plot he gave his name wrong. In a poignant slip he called himself not by his own name, John, but by his father's, Samuel. It is recorded that way in the burial register, and it is carved that way on the granite pillar at the south front of the cemetery, in gold letters.[32]

Wesley tried hard, then, to keep the Methodists single and celibate. But did they obey him? All indications are that they did not. They deferred to Wesley, and they loved him too; but one of the chief consequences of their attachment to him, as he himself saw, was that they came to be united with one another as well. In that close, deep, lasting union they found shared needs and views. Among the needs was cross-sex desire, and among the views, a strongly favorable outlook on marriage, which had come down to them from their Puritan forebears particularly and from Protestant tradition generally.[33] In union

[29]George J. Stevenson, *City Road Chapel, London, and Its Associations* (London, n.d.), p. 28.

[30]Curnock, 3: 30–31.

[31]Ibid., p. 31; George Stevenson, *Memorials of the Wesley Family* (New York, 1876), p. 227, prints the original inscription with two very slight differences. He has "Susanna" instead of "Susannah" and "youngest" instead of "the youngest."

[32]Stevenson, p. 227.

[33]On the strongly favorable Puritan outlook on marriage, the two fundamental essays are William and Malleville Haller, "The Puritan Art of Love," *Huntington Library Quarterly*, 5 (Jan. 1942): 235–72; and Edmund S. Morgan, Jr., "The Puritans and Sex," *New England Quarterly*, 15 (Dec. 1942): 591–607. On cross-sex desire in eighteenth-century England, see Henry Abelove, "Some Speculations on the History of 'Sexual Intercourse' During the 'Long Eighteenth Century' in England," *Genders*, 6 (Nov. 1989): 125–30.

they resisted Wesley's preference for celibacy, resisted also the pastoral arrangements he made to enforce it, and refused to let him be what maybe he wanted to be, the only marrying Methodist. Extramarital cross-sex intercourse they disapproved as strongly as Wesley could have wished. That they saw as definitely a sin. One Methodist, a London man, called it, perhaps with just a touch of complacency, his "reigning sin," but that it *was* a sin he simply took for granted.[34] Premarital cross-sex intercourse they also regarded generally as wrong, and a young Lancashire man, who spent a whole night together with his woman friend, would feel the need to explain even to his own diary that he had never taken his "Cloaths" off, that he had in no way "Brought Condemnation" on his "soul" by the "Nights Proceeding."[35] But toward marriage they felt differently, positively. It is true that very occasionally they hesitated about it on religious grounds, and one small group of Methodist men at Tetney actually made for themselves the sort of quasi-monastic community that Wesley most approved.[36] Ordinarily, though, they kept firmly to a position favoring marriage, and if a young society member was hesitating, scrupling about his own sexual wishes, he might be advised by an older, fellow Methodist, as one young Yorkshireman was, that his feelings were wholly natural: "He gave me to understand that I'd often taken that for lust which was rather an innocent Natural Effect

[34] Jos. Carter to Charles Wesley, 1741, Methodist Archive. Carter was writing of his pre-conversion days.

[35] Samuel Bardsley diary, Aug. 14, 1766, ibid. Bardsley is here describing an instance of what contemporaries sometimes called "bundling." For more on that practice, see Lawrence Stone, *The Family, Sex, and Marriage in England, 1500–1800* (New York, 1977), pp. 605–7.

[36] Curnock, 3: 281. This was the only such community Wesley ever reported that he found among the Methodists. But the eight early Shakers, who emigrated to the colony of New York in 1774, may have got their doctrine of celibacy—for which they were eventually to become so notorious—originally from Wesley. The group leader, Ann Lee, is known to have heard Whitefield preach and to have been much moved by him. She may have heard Wesley too. All eight came from the Manchester region, where Methodism was strong, and one may have actually been a society member. Edward Deming Andrews, *The People Called Shakers* (Oxford, 1953), pp. 7, 13; Hillel Schwartz, *The French Prophets* (Berkeley, Calif., 1980), p. 212. Oddly enough, Shakerism may have been the only true, large-scale development of Wesley's teaching on sex. On the rare instance of a Methodist's expressed hesitancy to marry for religious reasons, see Samuel Bardsley diary, July 14, 1766, Methodist Archive.

and had sometimes wish'd that destroying in me without which I could not long subsist."[37]

Probably they stood ready even to accept a certain measure of sexual intimacy between those who were engaged or near-engaged. A Methodist could write to his fiancée, who lived in another town, and ask that she arrange to have a private room available, where they could spend some time together undisturbed, either "at Mr. Atkinsons or at Mr. Smiths," both Methodist households, on the day he was planning to come for a visit.[38]

Such numerical evidence as may now be found tends to confirm that the Methodists resisted Wesley's pro-celibacy stance. For instance, a list is still extant, in Wesley's own handwriting, of the members of a society typical in many ways of Methodism generally, the Kingswood society. This list is dated 1757. It therefore shows what the society was after it had been under his pastoral oversight for about a generation. After each member's name Wesley indicated her or his address, occupation, and marital status. Of the 172 members in the society that year, only 31 were not, and had never been, married, and some of these were probably just children.[39] (There was no bar to admitting children to full membership in Methodism, and in fact they were encouraged to join.) If some were children, the proportion of members who were physically prepared to marry but had not done so was even smaller than 18 percent, maybe much smaller.[40] This was all the result that Wesley had of preaching and teaching celibacy at Kingswood for nearly a generation.

As for the pastoral arrangements that Wesley made for keeping the sexes apart, the Methodists resisted those too. His rule requiring separate seating at worship for men and women provoked much grumbling and at least two open showdowns, one between him and the Manchester society, the other between him and the London society.

---

[37]Thomas Illingworth diary, Jan. 18, 1756, Duke University Divinity School Library, Durham, N.C.

[38]Margaret M. Jemison, ed., *A Methodist Courtship* (Atlanta, Ga., 1945), p. 25.

[39]Kingswood society membership list, Pierpont Morgan Library, New York.

[40]In England generally, the nuptiality rate at this time was roughly 90 percent. Stone, p. 44. It is a reasonable guess, though I cannot substantiate it, that at least 90 percent of the members then on the society's list would marry during the course of their lifetimes.

But in his commitment to this rule Wesley was immovable. He won the showdown with the chapel committee of the London society in a "calm and loving consultation."[41] And he prevailed at Manchester by issuing his ultimate threat. "By jumbling men and women together," he told the society members, "you would shut me out of the house; for if I should come into a Methodist preaching house when this is the case, I must immediately go out again."[42]

If in resisting separate seating the Methodists were beaten back, they were more successful in resisting the bands and select-bands, the meetings for fellowship, segregated by sex, that Wesley had also arranged for them. A seating plan was something tangible, visible, controllable. Wesley could see that it was as he wished or order that it be redone. But the popularity of institutions like the bands and select-bands, the measure of emotional energy that went into them, was something intangible and diffuse, something that even Wesley could not control. Gradually, the Methodists let the bands and select-bands atrophy.[43]

These institutions did not disappear entirely. During Wesley's lifetime anyway, they continued to exist here and there. But even the relatively few that lasted were by no means so closed as Wesley wanted. They generated intimacy and secrets, but they could not always contain what they generated. For the members were typically thinking also of people excluded from the group, people of the opposite sex. Sometimes the members would have preferred to include these outsiders and told them about what was discussed inside. One Macclesfield woman, for instance, found that her fellow select-band-members had revealed her secrets to a man. As she wrote in her diary: "The Girls have been treacherous. . . . Are these they, whom I have Loved as my own Soul, to whom I have open'd the Secrets of my heart?—Ah My God—Where is Sincerity to be found? Where is Xtian friendship?"[44] In fact the institution for "Xtian friendship" the Methodists generally preferred, gave their energy to, and came to trust in was the one they had devised themselves in the early 1740's, the class. Unlike the band and select-band, the class was ordinarily

[41]Curnock, 7:349–50.
[42]Telford, *Letters*, 7:57.
[43]Baker, "Polity," p. 223.
[44]Hester Roe Rogers diary, Methodist Archive.

sexually mixed. It was based on neighborhood, and made up of a group of people who happened to live near to each other, including of course whole households and families. Every local society was divided into classes, and every class met weekly. Here at the class meetings, advice and reproof were exchanged, and spiritual experiences were discussed, just as at the meetings of the bands and select-bands, but in a format the Methodists were willing to favor and support: men and women together.[45]

As for Wesley's obvious reluctance to perform marriages, this the Methodists simply accepted. They could get their marriages done by their parish clergymen anyway. It was understood that their "good old Father" would be absent from the ceremony, even if he was traveling in the vicinity; and they did not hope for his participation, as they hoped that when they died, he might be there to bury them.[46]

They did not get to hear, Wesley did not get to tell them, why he was entitled to Grace Murray, why an exception to the celibacy policy was needed to join together the leader of Methodism and the most useful religious woman who had ever lived since the time of the crucifixion. They did, however, get to hear his rationale for marrying Mrs. Vazeille, his account of how by doing so he could quiet the scandalmongers. This rationale he delivered to various groups of the London society. Apparently he said nothing about caring for the woman. Instead he insisted that he felt marriage as a "cross" and was taking it up as a duty. One of the times he gave this statement, Charles was present, and he said that the people were so embarrassed by what they heard, they all hid their faces.[47]

Just as they were embarrassed by his rationale for marrying, so too they were embarrassed by his way of blanking out his parents' marriage. It was many years before they could or would do anything to rectify the inscription he had put on his mother's gravestone, but eventually, in 1828, after he had been safely dead for a little more than a generation, they took the stone down and set up a new one with a largely new inscription. In place of Wesley's "Here lies the body of

---

[45]Eventually class meetings too declined in popularity. But that happened much later, and in very different circumstances, approximately during the 1860's. See James Obelkevich, *Religion and Rural Society* (Oxford, 1976), p. 192.

[46]Curnock, 3: 199.

[47]Ibid., p. 515.

Mrs. Susannah Wesley, the Youngest and Last Surviving Daughter of Dr. Samuel Annesley," they put, "Here lies the body of Mrs. Susanna Wesley, Widow of the Rev. Samuel Wesley, M.A., late Rector of Epworth," and so restored to the woman her husband at last.[48] It was not until some years after this, in the mid-nineteenth century, that a Methodist antiquary found the name of "Samuel Wesley" in the cemetery register and on the pillar at the front of the cemetery. This error the antiquary wanted to rectify, too, and he enlisted the aid of the trustees of the cemetery, but they were unable to do anything about the pillar. "To correct an error deeply cut in granite," the antiquary said, "proved too difficult." Wesley's slip had to remain visibly there.[49]

Apparently Wesley got nowhere in his long campaign to induce celibacy in the Methodists. So far as the evidence shows, they continued to marry despite his teaching. But his pro-celibacy stance did make an impact on them. They did not accept it, did not in any sense follow it. Still, they heard it, attended to it, and may have found sanction in it for acting on certain needs of their own, needs that their union with each other greatly magnified. To sum up the matter briefly, there is some evidence to show that they found sanction in what Wesley said for devaluing and even breaking the family ties that troubled them; for releasing same-sex sexual feeling; and possibly also for practicing abstinence, within marriage, at the wife's insistence, as a means of birth control.

It should perhaps be added immediately that Wesley did not say that he approved of the devaluing and breaking of family ties, did not say that he approved of the release of same-sex sexual feeling, did not say that he approved of birth control based on abstinence. On the contrary he condemned all these practices. But he did present marriage as a second-best option, and by so doing he gave implied assent to what he otherwise explicitly opposed. The devaluing and breaking of family ties, same-sex eroticism, the refusal at the wife's insistence of marital sex: these were alternatives to a close marriage as then ideally conceived. His followers understood him as they wished, as they needed to, and they heard his implied assent far more distinctly than his explicit condemnation.

[48]Stevenson, *Memorials*, p. 228. This new inscription was paid for by the Wesleyan Book Committee.
[49]Ibid., p. 227.

For women particularly Methodism presented a unique opportunity to modify the family obligations that they felt to be oppressive. First, there was the continuous call to meetings: prayer meetings, class meetings, lovefeasts, watch-nights.[50] All these meetings took time, and to attend them was at the very least to escape from household drudgery. But the meetings might provide far more than escape. They might provide a recentering of the whole emotional life. Second, then, there was the continuous potential for developing commitments that might partly or even wholly replace those at home that felt burdensome. Along with these opportunities, and making them especially available, was the sanction provided by Wesley's implicit devaluation of marriage and of family.

What frightened contemporaries about Methodism, as much as anything else, was the opening it provided to women. In the polemics against Methodism this issue came up often. As the *Gentleman's Magazine* reported with outrage, "Many silly women" from among the ranks of the poor were attending Methodist meetings "every Morning" and leaving "their children in Bed till their Return, which sometimes is not til nine o'Clock . . . without any Regard to the grand Inconveniences, to which they are exposed by such neglect, contrary to the Laws of Nature."[51] Similarly, the riot against the Methodists at Wednesbury in Staffordshire, perhaps the most destructive of all the anti-Methodist riots of the eighteenth century, was sparked by a woman's temporary disappearance. "The wife of a certain Collier," the chronicler of the riot explained, "was missing from his House about a Week, without any Difference between him and her, and was found by him at one of the Class-houses."[52]

Methodist women were threatened, then, with stern reminders

[50]During this period Old Dissent, by contrast, was sponsoring relatively fewer special meetings. Horton Davies, *Worship and Theology in England, 1690–1850* (Princeton, N.J., 1961), p. 111.

[51]*Gentleman's Magazine*, 11 (June 1741): 320. See also, for instance, Francis Place's comment on his sister's married life during the 1780's. She and her husband were unhappy together. "He therefore sought for consolation in drinking and she in methodism. She went to chapel, prayed, and sung hymns at home, and was as absurd as he was, she held some office in the religious community to which she belonged, and used to attend meetings when she ought to have been at home." Mary Thrale, ed., *The Autobiography of Francis Place* (Cambridge, Eng., 1972), p. 93.

[52]*Some Papers Giving an Account of the Rise and Progress of Methodism at Wednesbury in Staffordshire and other Parishes Adjacent* (London, 1744), p. 21.

about "the Laws of Nature" and even with riot. Sometimes they also got personal letters of counsel, half-solicitous, half-menacing. One Chester girl, young, still unmarried and living with her parents, got such a letter from the vicar of the parish. Her mother had told the vicar that the girl had been attending Methodist meetings when she ought to have been doing household chores. Pronouncing himself "shocked and surprized," he wrote: "It gives me much concern to hear that you have given any part of the time which ought to be faithfully and conscientiously employed in discharging the common duties of life, to an attendance upon a set of men who call themselves Methodists." The Methodists, he added, never failed to bring "confusion and disorder among families." He warned her that the chores and the bonds she was escaping from were ordained for her of God, and he referred to Scripture as his warrant for saying so: "St. Paul tells us that if a man will not work, neither must he eat; that those who neglect their own households are worse than infidels." Finally, he tried intimidation. He said that if she should "desert the duties of that state of life" to which God had been pleased to call her, then he, as vicar of the parish, would "recommend it strongly" to her mother to throw her out of the house altogether.[53]

Despite appeals to the laws of nature, the danger of riot, and threats, women continued to find scope in Methodism for devaluing and breaking the ties they disliked. They could reorient their lives away from the household, could get away—to some extent physically, and perhaps to a greater extent emotionally—from what one Methodist woman called a "cruel husband" or from parents who were what another called "God's enemies."[54] If women particularly found such an escape in Methodism, men found it as well. They were less bound, of course, to the household and felt less need to escape from it physically. But Wesley's tacit undercutting of marriage and family freed them too, and enabled them to turn away emotionally from their families as they wished. They found sanction for saying, and

[53]Francis Bretherton, *Early Methodism in and around Chester 1749–1812* (Chester, 1903), pp. 101–2.
[54]Margaret Austin to Charles Wesley, May 19, 1740, Methodist Archive; Joseph Beaumont, *Memoirs of Mrs. Mary Tatham, Late of Nottingham* (New York, 1839), p. 41. Some women even preached. See Deborah Valenze, *Prophetic Sons and Daughters* (Princeton, N.J., 1985), pp. 50–54. But this was relatively uncommon during Wesley's lifetime.

feeling, as one Cornishman put it, "They that love the Lord are nearer to me than my carnal relations."[55] Most often the men who felt oppressed were eager to break with their fathers, and they could easily use their Methodism to catalyze the break. One young man forced a showdown with his father, left the house, and moved in with his uncles, who were also Methodists.[56] Another, a Cornishman, got kicked out, moved in with neighbors, and went into business with them.[57] A third, a Yorkshireman, made his break only after his father died. He had his father's tombstone read, as in his father's voice:[58]

> Death hath summon'd me,
> and I must appear,
> Before the bar of God,
> my doom to hear.

From the very start of the movement, even in the days when Methodism was still just a club at Oxford, the Methodists had shown a quick and unconventional sympathy with same-sex eroticism. They had then, in 1732, rather ostentatiously taken the part of a man named Blair, who had been convicted of sodomy. Their support for this man had apparently raised eyebrows throughout the university. As one non-Methodist clerical observer commented, "Whether the man is innocent or no they were not proper judges, it was better he should suffer than such a scandal given on countenancing a man whom the whole town think guilty of such an enormous crime." Then he added, "Whatever good design they pretend it was highly imprudent and has given the occasion of terrible reflections."[59]

[55] James Chubb journal, July 13, 1782, Methodist Archive.
[56] Cecil Driver, *Tory Radical* (Oxford, 1946), p. 5.
[57] Richard Treffrey, *Memoirs of Mr. Richard Trewavas, Sr., of Mousehole Cornwall* (London, 1839), pp. 57–61.
[58] Richard Burdsall, *Memoirs of the Life of Richard Burdsall* (3d ed.; Thetford, Eng., 1823), p. 155.
[59] C. S. Linnell, ed., *Diaries of Thomas Wilson, D.D.* (London, 1964), p. 81. This incident is noticed by V. H. H. Green, *John Wesley* (London, 1964), p. 32. Wilson is apparently referring to male-male sex, though the term "sodomy" in eighteenth-century English usage can in some contexts mean other things as well. For an account of the very severe attitude commonly taken toward male-male sex in eighteenth-century England, see Randolph Trumbach, "London's Sodomites," *Journal of Social*

Presumably the "terrible reflections" were that sodomy was a Methodist practice. If that was the guess the Oxonians were making, they may have been wrong. It is now probably impossible to know. On the one hand, there is virtually no verbal evidence of sodomy in any of the early Methodists' confessional diaries, journals, or letters, thousands of which are still extant. On the other hand, a Methodist who was practicing sodomy would have had good reason to keep the matter quiet. What is clear is that the conditions of Methodist group life provided an opening for some same-sex sexual feeling, and at the ᵃme time Wesley's undercutting of family and marriage provided a sanction. In fact the Methodists came to be unusually tender, men with men, women with women, and their interest in Blair could well have been based on a fellow feeling warmer than charity.

Their physical demonstrativeness with those of their own sex certainly included kissing. They kissed at highly wrought religious scenes, as, for instance, at the big revival at Everton, when the newly converted went around the room kissing "all of their own sex."[60] But their tenderness was probably prompted less by experiences like that, which were occasional, than by the ongoing pastoral arrangements that Wesley had made for them. These arrangements—separate seating at worship, bands and select-bands, the continuous exhorting to stay single—they resisted, but they also lived with. They found themselves often thrown together intimately, men with men, women with women, and they responded to each other. It was easy to respond, too. As one Methodist said of the men friends with whom he met in band, "Their experience answered to mine as face to face in a glass."[61]

Sometimes they not only responded but actually fell in love. These love affairs were sweet but also painful and awkward, and they typically produced sharp jealousies, maybe because they were unrequited. One Macclesfield woman, Mrs. Stonehewer, fell in love with her neighbor and fellow Methodist, Hester Roe, and almost immediately

---

History, 11 (1977): 11–22. See also George S. Rousseau, "The Pursuit of Homosexuality in the Eighteenth Century," in Robert Parks Maccubin, *'Tis Nature's Fault* (Cambridge, Eng., 1987), pp. 132–68.

[60]Curnock, 4: 320. For a similar kissing incident, see Jackson, 1: 153.

[61]*Life of Henry Longden, Minister of the Gospel* (New York, 1837), p. 39. On women's bands, see Gail Malmgreen, "Domestic Discords," in Jim Obelkevich, Lyndal Roper, and Raphael Samuel, eds., *Disciplines of Faith* (London, 1987), p. 60.

began to suffer from the fear that Hester cared more for her sister, also a Methodist, than for herself. Hester's diary is the source of our knowledge of the affair. There, in the diary, Hester portrays herself as an unwilling participant in this triangle, as feeling for the unhappy Mrs. Stonehewer and the sister, too, just friendship and no more. It is plain enough, though, from what Hester says, that she was to some extent inviting the feeling that Mrs. Stonehewer felt for her.

The scene opens with Hester's noting that she had just got a message from Mrs. Stonehewer, saying that "she was so Unhappy lest I shD Love her sister more than her that she had no rest." Hester sent back a message assuring Mrs. Stonehewer of friendship, yet warning her against "expecting in the Creature what alone is to be found in God." Two days after this another message came to Hester: Mrs. Stonehewer was "distress'd" with fears that Hester did not love her. They met later that day, and Mrs. Stonehewer asked Hester to leave the class she was then affiliated with, because her sister would be meeting there, too, and to join Mrs. Stonehewer's own class. Hester refused, and Mrs. Stonehewer got upset: "When I told her I cD not possibly, she was much tried and left me in very low spirits—Lord . . . Be thou the one Object of her Love." The next day Mrs. Stonehewer threatened to resign from the Methodist society altogether if Hester did not switch classes. Hester still refused, praying that "the Lord wD make" Mrs. Stonehewer remain a Methodist and would also "wean her from this inordinate affection for me."

Later in the week Mrs. Stonehewer backed down from her threat, said that she would stay a Methodist. She also appeared less infatuated than before. Hester observed: "Her Affection for me seem'd more Consistent.— . . . I took her upstairs—." While upstairs, Hester "conversed and went to prayer wTH her—and had much Liberty and she seem'd greatly encouraged." But a few weeks after this removal upstairs, Mrs. Stonehewer was again much distressed and talked to Hester of suicide. Hester responded by dealing "freely and plainly with her yet affectionately." That is the last glimpse the diary affords of their relationship.[62]

Men as well as women fell into these loves. One man named John Hutchinson, in his early twenties apparently, fell in love with Charles.

[62]Hester Roe Rogers diary, Methodist Archive.

Since John lived in Leeds, and Charles at that time in Bristol, John wrote him letters. Two of them are still extant. In the first of the letters John wrote:

Dear Sir *I cannot describe how I love you*, my Heart is ready to break that Providence hath allotted *me to be So far Separate from* you, I could live and die with you. . . . Write to me often and love me more, let *no new Convert be my Rival*, continue your loving Kindness unto me and admit *no one to have* a greater share in your affection than your poor unworthy ungrateful Young Man. I have been broken-hearted ever since your Departure.

Then, later in that same letter, he commented on the letter he had lately received from Charles. It struck him as insufficiently warm:

Upon first Sight of your Letter my Heart leaped for Joy, I have read it over Times without Number, but cannot find your accustomed Manner of writing, (wch was), *dear Johnny, dear Youth*. . . . I remember in your three Letters to Mr. Shent, you begun with dear William, don't be angry at my Simplicity, it is a weakness I cannot help, (what shall I say) in my own Strength I can promise nothing, but according to the present Situation of my Mind, I desire I may cease to breathe when I foresake you, you are dearer to me than myself and you shall never want anything I can do for you only continue *to travel and I will work for your Support*.[63]

That was the first of John's surviving letters. In the second, written about a year later, he made a new suggestion for bringing the two of them together. Previously he had written of working to support Charles; now he proposed that he come to Charles's house at Bristol and board there. He thought he could never be a good Christian until he was there close to Charles:

I continue yet very irreligious and think I shall never be better *until I make my abode with you*. I have some Thoughts, as I entirely Dislike to live at Leeds, to come and *live at Bristol* as soon as I can be disengaged from Business wch will not be before the Expiration of 2 Years, if please God so long to spare me, will you let *me board with you*. . . .[64]

Of these two letters the first bears a superscription in Charles's own handwriting, his commentary on the affair. It is a Latin tag: "Uno avulso non deficit alter." This was the motto of the Austrian imperial

---

[63] John Hutchinson to Charles Wesley, Sept. 29, 1751, ibid.
[64] John Hutchinson to Charles Wesley, Sept. 10, 1752, ibid.

house. It referred to the emblem of the house, the two-headed eagle, and it may be translated as "One torn away, another takes its place." What Charles obviously meant by quoting the tag was that John's attitude was nothing very new. Some other man also had recently been in love with him.[65]

Historians now generally agree that family planning by various means was occasionally practiced in eighteenth-century England. They usually suppose that the means used were coitus interruptus, coitus reservatus, abortion, and infanticide or neglect amounting to infanticide.[66] Among the Methodists another means may possibly have been used, too: long-term conjugal abstinence at the wife's insistence. Here the evidence is scanty and uncertain. But to say at once what may be true but cannot now be proved, the Methodist women who felt that they had attained what they called Perfection, freedom from all inward sin, may have refused ever after to have sex with their husbands.

This hypothesis would make sense of the remark an observant non-Methodist made about "double-ribbed" women among the Methodists.[67] It would also make sense of the rumor that one London Methodist heard concerning "some women" in the society, that they were refusing "to sleep with their husbands."[68] It might even make sense of a certain feature of the seating arrangement at the London Foundery. Throughout most of the room the seats were plain, backless benches. But in a little area just underneath the pulpit, there were a few benches with back-rails. These seats of dignity were evidently

[65]David Hilliard, "UnEnglish and Unmanly," *Victorian Studies*, 25 (Winter 1982): 181–210, makes a rather comparable point about nineteenth-century Anglo-Catholicism: that with its emphasis on the value of celibacy, it may have been particularly attractive to some homosexuals. I want to thank Philip Jones for bringing this essay to my attention.

[66]E. A. Wrigley, "Family Limitation in Pre-Industrial England," in Orest and Patricia Ranum, eds., *Popular Attitudes Toward Birth Control in Pre-Industrial France and England* (New York, 1972), especially pp. 91–92. But family planning became *common* only during the nineteenth century. E. A. Wrigley and R. S. Schofield, *The Population History of England* (London, 1981), pp. 427, 479.

[67]John Cass to Thomas Wride, July 23, 1779, Methodist Archive.

[68]Lackington, p. 160.

intended for holy women, their holiness being somehow represented by their closeness to the preacher and by their straight backs.[69] Certainly, the Methodist women were as frightened as were the Englishwomen of their era generally about the pains and risks of childbearing. One of them, while pregnant and close to term, confessed to Wesley that she was "greatly afraid" that she would "die in labour," and although she survived, her fear was of course realistic.[70] Another woman, a London Methodist, wrote a full account of her feelings about childbearing, a rare and moving document. "I had uncommon Suffering in child-bearing," she noted, "which kept me in continual fear." Because of her sufferings and fear, she eventually felt inclined to abort one of her pregnancies. This inclination struck her as a temptation of the devil:

The Enemie took advantage of my weakness and when I had conceived of my 5th child [enticed] me to use some means to disappoint God's Providence in bringing it to perfection, and that way free my Self from the Pain I so much dreaded. Sometimes I thought it would be Murder. He answerd, No, that as yet there was no life.[71]

In this time of temptation, God, she said, helped her. She overcame and bore the child.

For a woman like this, who "dreaded" the pains and risks of repeated childbearing, and whose husband was apparently unwilling to help her by practicing coitus interruptus or coitus reservatus or maybe anal or oral intercourse, and was instead determined on the one kind of intercourse that could lead to reproduction (penis in vagina, vagina around penis, with seminal emission uninterrupted), abortion was of course an option, and it is no wonder that it occurred to her. But she was close to conventional religious sentiment and disapproved strongly of her own thoughts about abortion. That way out was blocked. In her view it would have been "murder." With that way

---

[69]Stevenson, *City Road Chapel*, p. 20.

[70]Curnock, 5: 236.

[71]Mrs. Clagett memorandum, July 24, 1738, Methodist Archive. My reading of "enticed" is a guess. At that point I find the manuscript illegible. Eventually, Mrs. Clagett turned Moravian, and it is interesting to note that, according to a report Wesley himself circulated, the Moravians permitted even abortion. Curnock, 4: 7.

blocked there was very little left for her, if she was determined to keep herself from pregnancy, except abstinence. It is true that abstinence, at least abstinence at the insistence of just the wife and against the wishes of the husband, was as forbidden religiously as abortion. Here, however, Wesley's preference for celibacy may have helped her. It may have prompted her to think about the possibility of living for the future without sex, and it may have been taken by her as a sanction for doing so. Besides, she was part of a group, a unified and mutually loving group that included many women who were in a predicament like hers. Their need would have reinforced hers, and she and they together may have taught themselves to understand Wesley in a way that made sense to them, in a way that accorded with their wishes.[72]

Wesley taught celibacy, but the Methodists learned something different. Except for a very few of them, like the small group at Tetney that he so much approved of, there was nothing for them in celibacy, nothing they commonly wanted. Resisting the actual content of his teaching, they married and made love as English people usually did. Still, they adored Wesley and wanted to do as he asked. His pro-celibacy stand may have been unpalatable, but it may have made an impact on them anyway and may have helped them to feel wants that they shared and that they could act on satisfactorily to themselves. If they followed him, it was in their own way.[73]

These features of early Methodism—Wesley's pro-celibacy stance, the dimensions of the popular response to it—have long been suppressed in historical memory. In the eighteenth-century world the Methodists lived in, these features were at least inchoately known. Their contemporaries certainly understood this much: that Methodism somehow represented an undercutting of family life as conventionally ordered. One proof that they so understood Methodism

[72]Randolph Trumbach, *The Rise of the Egalitarian Family* (New York, 1978), p. 175, notes the case of a married woman who decided on abstinence as a means of family planning and convinced herself that the abstinence was religiously right.

[73]It will be plain that I cannot endorse, without important qualification, Lawrence Stone's judgment that in practice evangelicalism led to sexual "repression" and "the crushing of the libido." *Family*, pp. 645, 678. This judgment relies overmuch on leaders like Wesley as indices of the movement.

may be found in their lurid fantasizing about Dionysiac excesses, unspeakable orgies, at society-rooms and lovefeasts.[74] Another proof may be found in the amazing circumstance that prostitutes sometimes moved into Methodist preaching-houses and set up living quarters there. In 1776 Wesley had to issue a formal order demanding that these prostitutes, or "sluts" as he called them, be driven out.[75] If contemporaries understood Methodism, so did the Methodists themselves. They knew what they were doing, knew the risks, the dangers, the troubles. It is no wonder that a favorite metaphor of theirs for the Methodist movement was "the hospital."[76] But they knew also their pleasures and satisfactions, and they talked often, especially among themselves, of the sweetness of their fellowship.

[74]For a summary account of the attacks on Methodism for orgiastic excess, see Albert Lyles, *Methodism Mocked* (London, 1960), pp. 90–93. John Walsh views these attacks as "paranoid." See his "Methodism and the Mob in the Eighteenth Century," in G. J. Cuming and Derek Baker, eds., *Popular Belief and Practice* (Cambridge, Eng., 1972), pp. 224–25.

[75]*Minutes of the Methodist Conferences* (London, 1862), 1: 126.

[76]See, for instance, Susan Brooke, "Journal of Isabella MacKiver," *Proceedings of the Wesley Historical Society*, 28 (March 1952): 159–63; and Eliza Weaver Bradburn, *Memoirs of the Late Rev. Samuel Bradburn* (London, 1816), p. 20.

Chapter Six

Spirituality

Wesley taught the Methodists no particular theology, no particular inflection of the Christian tradition. Instead he provided them with an internally contradictory mix of virtually everything Christian, new and old, Protestant and Catholic, Dissenting and Anglican, heretical and orthodox. The points he emphasized in his teaching at any given moment depended principally on what he was then opposing. For he was always concerned to distinguish his position from something or other else, to keep the attention of his flock fixed firmly on himself.

Take his teaching on justification. In the early stages of his career as a traveling evangelist, he taught clearly and unequivocally that justification was by faith alone. At that time he was a Church of England clergyman just starting to attract a following. His peers, his competitors, were his fellow parsons, most of whom preached to their parishioners of duty and morals. To assert himself in contradistinction to them, he needed to put his Reformation side forward. Certainly he had a Reformation side, all the more securely after his various contacts with the German pietists during the 1730's and after his conversion experience in 1738, and he could emphasize that side without any falseness. He said repeatedly in those early years that "faith alone" made the way to "justification," or in the technical language of theology, that "the death and righteousness of Christ" were the only "meritorious cause" of "justification," and that "faith" was the only "conditional or instrumental" cause.[1]

[1]Nehemiah Curnock, ed., *The Journal of the Rev. John Wesley, A.M.* (London, 1909–16), 2: 262.

But he went further than that. He said that before his conversion and his various contacts with the German pietists, when he had lived by his regimen of good works and preached justification by faith and works, he had been without knowing it "fundamentally" a "Papist."[2] Here the implication was clear. If Wesley had once been very wrong, he now was right. Anybody else who remained wrong in that way, who still preached up faith and works, was virtually a Catholic. This was a powerful innuendo.

Naturally, questions arose among Wesley's excited followers and helpers as they heard him drive home the Reformation doctrine. They especially wanted to know about works that preceded the onset of faith, "works," as they said, "meet for repentance." Were these works necessary to the process of justification? And if so, were they not a condition of justification, as much as faith was?

In 1744 Wesley summoned some of his colleagues to a conference, at which these questions and others were allowed to surface. As the questions were asked, Wesley answered them. Later he published minutes of the exchange in pamphlet form. "We began," he explained in the pamphlet, "with considering the doctrine of justification." He then listed the questions that had been put relating to that doctrine and "the substance of the answers given thereto":

Q. 1. What is to be justified?
A. To be pardoned, and received into God's favour, into such a state that, if we continue therein we shall be finally saved.
Q. 2. Is faith the condition of justification?
A. Yes; for everyone who believeth not is condemned; and everyone who believes is justified.

Then came the question that obviously concerned his colleagues most:

Q. 3. But must not repentance and works meet for repentance go before this faith?

Wesley's answer was:

A. Without doubt: if by repentance you mean conviction of sin; and by works meet for repentance, obeying God as far as we can, forgiving

[2]Ibid.

our brother, leaving off from evil, doing good, and using His ordinances according to the power we have received.[3]

This answer was satisfactory so far as it went, but Wesley's colleagues still wanted to know why the "works meet for repentance" should not be considered a "condition" of justification, just as faith was. In the following year, 1745, they met again for another conference (from this time on, the conference was to be an annual event), and the first item of business that was "proposed" was to "review the minutes of the last Conference with regard to justification." Then the questions came, sharper and more impatient in tone than the year before:

Q. 1. How comes what is written on this subject to be so intricate and obscure? Is this obscurity from the nature of the thing itself? Or, from the fault or weakness of those who have generally treated of it?
A.   We apprehend this obscurity does not arise from the nature of the subject: but, perhaps partly from hence, that the devil peculiarly labours to perplex a subject of the greatest importance; and partly from the extreme warmth of most writers who have treated of it.
Q. 2. We affirm faith in Christ is the sole condition of justification. But does not repentance go before that faith? Yea, and (supposing there be opportunity for them) fruits or works meet for repentance?
A.   Without doubt they do.

Finally, the point at issue:

Q. 3. How then can we deny them to be conditions of justification? Is not this a mere strife of words? But is it worth while to continue a dispute on the term condition?

Wesley conceded:

A.   It seems not, though it has been grievously abused. But so the abuse cease, let the use remain.[4]

To ease his colleagues' puzzlement Wesley was willing, at least when pressed repeatedly, to relinquish his preference for calling just faith and nothing else a "condition" of justification. No good would come of irritable quarrels about a mere term like "condition." They might, if they wished, talk of works meet for repentance as a "con-

[3]*Minutes of the Methodist Conferences* (London, 1862), 1: 1.
[4]Ibid., pp. 6–7.

dition" of justification, provided that they remembered that Christ would extend his pardon just to believers.

That was in 1745, when Wesley was still in the first stages of his great life work, when he was just starting to make a name for himself and striving hard to distinguish his outlook from his fellow parsons'. A generation later the situation was different. By then Wesley was fully established in the public view, and he was known as the leader of a great movement. He employed scores of lay preachers, controlled hundreds of preaching-houses, and cared for a flock of members and adherents numbering far into the thousands. If he looked like anything any way familiar, he looked like a separatist, a leader of Dissent. By then his natural competitors were no longer the moralizing parsons of the earlier days; his competitors were the evangelicals, some of whom were Dissenters, some of whom were still like him precariously within the church.

In the period of the late 1760's, and throughout the decade of the 1770's, his evangelical competitors were chiefly "the striplings who call themselves lady Huntingdon's preachers." They were the ones who were trying "to divide" his "poor little flock,"[5] and they were true-blue reformers. To distinguish himself from them, Wesley was obliged to put his Catholic side forward. Certainly he had a Catholic side, just as he had a Reformation side. At Oxford and even after, he had been on his own testimony virtually a "Papist." Although that was a polemical exaggeration, his affinities with the Catholic tradition of holiness were real enough. So at the conference of 1770 he recast his position on justification by faith. He said, peremptorily:

Review the whole affair.

1. Who of us is *now* accepted of God?
   He that believes in Christ, with a loving, obedient heart.

2. But who among those that never heard of Christ?
   He that feareth God, and worketh righteousness, according to the light that he has.

3. Is this the same with "he that is sincere?"
   Nearly, if not quite.

[5]Curnock, 6: 241–42. At the time the preachers of Lady Huntingdon's Connection were still within the church. They made what they considered to be their decisive break in 1783.

4. Is not this "salvation by works?"
Not by the *merit* of works, but by works as a condition.

Note that here Wesley insisted on what previously he had barely been willing to allow, the description of works as a "condition" of justification. He then added:

5. What have we then been disputing about for these thirty years? I am afraid, about words.

To cap the whole, he said also:

6. As to *merit* itself, of which we have been so dreadfully afraid: we are rewarded "according to our *works*," yea, "because of our works." How does this differ from *for the sake of our works*? And how differs this from *secundem merita operum*,—as our works *deserve*? Can you split this hair? I doubt I cannot.[6]

With that Wesley distinguished himself sufficiently from the other evangelicals around him. In fact he provoked an uproar, as doubtless he intended. At the following year's conference, a delegation of Lady Huntingdon's preachers waited on him in a body to demand a recantation or an explanation. When they arrived, he placidly assured them that he was still as much a proponent of justification by faith alone as ever he had been, that his views were the same presently as previously, and that he had been preaching the everlasting gospel for more than thirty years.[7] After some further discussion, Wesley persuaded the befuddled leader of the delegation to say that he must have misunderstood the meaning of the previous year's published minutes. That acknowledged, Wesley permitted the delegation to withdraw.

Take also Wesley's teaching about the depravity of humankind. He said often that in his view the most dangerously prevalent heresy of the day was the denial of original sin. He found this heresy at Shackerley, in Ireland, in a book printed in Geneva, "without any hindrance or animadversion."[8] He found it cropping up here and

[6]*Minutes of Conferences*, 1: 95–96.

[7]Wesley gave the substance of this assurance in writing. See Luke Tyerman, *The Life and Times of the Rev. John Wesley, A.M.* (London, 1870–72), 3: 100. For a recent effort to give consistency to Wesley's teaching on justification, see Frederick Dreyer, "Faith and Experience in the Thought of John Wesley," *American Historical Review*, 88 (Feb. 1983): 12–30.

[8]Curnock, 3: 374; 5: 308; 4: 200.

there among the clergy of Europe, in the universities, and even among the people. Wherever he traveled, whatever he read, there was evidence of the spreading "poison."⁹ So far as he could tell, the source of the heresy, in the form in which it was then spreading, was the writings of a Norwich Dissenter, Dr. John Taylor. Wesley confided to a correspondent that Taylor had probably inflicted the worst "wound" on Christianity of any "single person since Mahomet."¹⁰ To combat Taylor and to defend "the whole frame of Scriptural Christianity,"¹¹ Wesley wrote a book reasserting the doctrine of original sin and begged Taylor to reply, so that the debate between them might be carried to a full conclusion. In the letter begging for the reply, Wesley said to Taylor, "Either I or you mistake the whole of Christianity from the beginning to the end."¹²

Yet even as he was attacking Taylor for his heresy and begging for a reply to the attack, Wesley was preaching among believers, and among believers only, that if they prayed and watched and hoped, they could expect to be freed during their lifetimes from all sin, even original sin. This total freedom from sin Wesley called appropriately enough, Perfection.¹³ To the unawakened he said nothing about it, and to those whom he suspected of following Taylor's views, he insisted "much more than" he was "accustomed to do on the doctrine of Original Sin."¹⁴ But to justified Christians Wesley explained that they could go another step beyond pardon; that God was willing to grant them release from all evil thoughts and evil tempers; that he would do so in an instant, maybe long before their deaths; and that this instantaneous gift would destroy in them entirely "the evil root, the carnal mind."¹⁵

⁹Ibid., 4: 200.
¹⁰John Telford, ed., *The Letters of the Rev. John Wesley, A.M.* (London, 1931), 4: 48.
¹¹Curnock, 3: 374.
¹²Ibid., 4: 328.
¹³John Wesley, *A Plain Account of Christian Perfection* (London, 1820). I refer to the printing designated as 12 in Frank Baker, *Union Catalogue of the Publications of John and Charles Wesley* (Durham, N.C., 1966), p. 125. Wesley used the term "entire sanctification" interchangeably with Perfection.
¹⁴Curnock, 3: 520.
¹⁵Quoted by Harald Lindström, *Wesley and Sanctification* (Stockholm, 1946), p. 145.

Welsey took pains to stipulate that when Perfect morally, they would still have their bodily and mental defects, whatever those happened to be. Neither "ungracefulness of pronunciation" nor "slowness of understanding" and the mistakes arising from it would vanish in the Perfect.[16] But their "hearts" and "hands" would be wholly "cleansed." "Inbred sin" would subsist in them no more; the "leprosy" would be healed.[17]

It may be that nothing quite like Wesley's notion of Perfection had been preached in Christendom before. It is true that Kempis, Francis de Sales, and the Syrian monks of the fifth century had all thought of the religious life as a gradual process of sanctification, leading to an ever-increasing purity of intention, and culminating in glorification. But for them the full attainment of perfection came only with death. It is also true that the reformers of the sixteenth century had written of perfection. Generally, they had held that perfection in faith could come during the Christian's lifetime but moral perfection could come only with death.[18] Wesley's doctrine, that the "leprosy" could be healed in this world, was probably new. "This doctrine," as he himself explained, was "the grand depositum" that God had "lodged with the people called Methodists."[19]

Naturally, the teaching of Perfection aroused wonder, as for instance in the Leeds Dissenter who, after listening to some Methodists talking of it, recorded in his diary that he had never been "taught" anything like it "before."[20] It also aroused opposition, and one of the earlier opponents was a young man named Richard Tompson, a one-

[16] Wesley, *Plain Account*, pp. 17–18.

[17] Quoted by Lindström, p. 145.

[18] I follow the very careful distinctions made in ibid., pp. 127–37. On Wesley's interest in the Syrian monks, see Albert Outler, ed., *John Wesley* (New York, 1964), pp. 9–10. As the text suggests, I do not see anything strictly comparable to Wesley's Perfection even in the radical Puritans, who are often characterized as having maintained Perfectionism. Note the relevant passages quoted from the radical Puritans by G. Nuttall, *The Holy Spirit in Puritan Faith and Experience* (Oxford, 1946), pp. 54–55, 157; and by Christopher Hill, *The World Turned Upside Down* (New York, 1972), pp. 65–68, 130–31.

[19] Telford, *Letters*, 7: 238.

[20] He also wrote that he found no "ground to take it in." This was Joseph Ryder, and the entry was for March 5, 1745. Parts of the diary, including this part, are published in Herbert McLachlan, *Essays and Addresses* (Manchester, 1950), p. 33.

time Methodist who, after he had left the flock, engaged Wesley in an extended theological correspondence, which was eventually published. Concerning Perfection, Tompson wrote:

I can hardly think, Sir, that you have sufficiently attended to the Consequences which necessarily follow from this doctrine: As suppose, for instance, that two persons *absolutely free from the Corruption of human nature* should marry and have Children; it is very evident that they could convey no Corruption of Nature to their Offspring, nor they to theirs; even to the remotest Generations: And therefore this *new Species* of Mankind would stand in no need of a Savior.[21]

To this thrust Wesley replied shortly: "As to Christian Perfection, I believe Two who were made perfect in Love, never did, or will, marry together."[22] Practically, Wesley may have been right. He apparently knew or guessed that women were using Perfection to veer away from marital sexuality. But theologically, his answer was of course evasive.

Tompson then pressed him again. "As 'Marriage is honourable in *all*,'" he wrote, quoting the New Testament,

I cannot see why two perfect Persons (supposing there were any such) might not marry now. I am sure the contrary can never be proved. But if it could, the difficulty is not one Jot removed: For the Question will still return. Suppose that two Persons, already married, should attain to such a state? The very same Consequences would inevitably follow, as on the Other Supposition. And I suppose you will hardly venture to affirm, that God will never make any married Couple (capable of having Children) perfect. If you did, I should ask you, *first*, What Ground you had for such an *arbitrary Hypothesis*? and *secondly*, How you came to marry yourself, when you judged it would be an infallible Means of keeping either *yourself*, or *your Wife* from that State which is of *all others* the most desirable?[23]

In response to all this Wesley was still more evasive. He made no reply whatever to anything Tompson said or asked about Perfection. His rebuttal was that his time was much "taken up," that he was a "slow"

---

[21] *Original Letters Between the Reverend John Wesley, and Mr. Richard Tompson, Respecting the Doctrine of Assurance* (London, 1760), p. 16.

[22] Ibid., p. 20. This passage is omitted in the standard edition of Wesley's letters. See Telford, *Letters*, 3: 137.

[23] *Original Letters*, p. 32. Tompson is referring to Heb. 13 : 4.

writer, and that what little he could manage to snatch time to write was necessarily written in "haste."[24]

Others, too, pressed Wesley hard about Perfection. One of the helpers wrote him a letter sterner than anything by Tompson. It is no longer extant, but Wesley described it as "peremptory" and "highly offensive," and noted that it included exclamations like "O horrid! O dreadful!," pointed apparently against the doctrine of Perfection. Along with these exclamations, the helper had also let drop the name of Pelagius, the fifth-century heretic who was thought to have denied original sin. This was to lay down the gauntlet with a vengeance, and Wesley replied, just as aggressively: "Who was Pelagius? By all I can pick up from ancient authors, I guess he was both a wise and an holy man."[25] He went on to advise the helper to avoid theological controversy for the future, telling him, "you have an honest heart, but not a clear head." He warned as well. To "get into controversy" would be to "invade the glories of our adorable King and the unspeakable rights and privileges and comforts of His children."[26]

Against the parsons, then, Wesley was a reformer; against the reformers, a parson. Against the heretics, the neo-Pelagians like Taylor and his followers, Wesley was a Christian; against the Christians, a proponent of Perfection and Pelagius. To his flock—and this of course was the point—he was unique, irreplaceable, mysterious, and almost unknowable. He was less like a preacher than like the God figured in the Scriptures of the Hebrews, the God whose attributes are all paradoxical and whose being is hidden. Once Wesley was present at a lovefeast, a special meeting of the flock held at night, where all were telling of their own spiritual experiences. While the others spoke, Wesley himself remained silent. One of the flock, doubtless somebody especially brave, "rose up, and addressing himself to Mr. Wesley said, 'Sir, I am persuaded that it would be very gratifying to the friends present to hear your *experience*, and espe-

---

[24]Ibid., pp. 34, 6. This correspondence ended in 1756. Ten years later Wesley gave a theological answer to the questions Tompson had raised: "Sin is entailed upon me, not by immediate generation, but my first parent," Adam. He still maintained that a marriage between two Perfect persons was not "probable." Wesley, *Plain Account*, p. 61.

[25]Telford, *Letters*, 4: 158. This was by no means the only time that, attacked about Perfection, Wesley stood up for Pelagius. See also, for instance, ibid., 6: 175.

[26]Ibid., 4: 158.

cially *your views* of entire Sanctification.'" At that, so the report of the incident goes: "Mr. Wesley instantly stood up, and said, with great solemnity of manner and voice, 'By the grace of God, I am what I am.' He then sat down; and after a short pause, the speaking was resumed."[27]

Along with the contradictory emphases in his teaching of the two basic Christian doctrines of justification and depravity, Wesley provided his flock with a medley of publications designed to acquaint them with the great thinkers and personages of the Christian past. He gave them excerpts from Pascal and the life of a New Englander, David Brainerd; accounts of the martyrdoms of Polycarp and Ignatius and of the life of the Spanish mystic Gregory Lopez; an antislavery essay by the Quaker Anthony Benezet; passages from Bunyan's *Holy War*; big selections from Foxe's *Book of Martyrs* and the latitudinarian sermons of John Tillotson; the devotional exercises of the French mystic Antoinette Bourignon; several tracts by the Puritan Thomas Goodwin; a set of the religious poems of the Anglican George Herbert; an edition of Henry Brooke's sentimental novel *The Fool of Quality*; an abridgment of Milton's *Paradise Lost*; some of Edward Young's *Night Thoughts*; the writings of the fifth-century Syrian monk Macarius; and an edition of Samuel Johnson's novella *Rasselas*. Much of this material Wesley collected into a fifty-volume set that he called "the Christian Library," and he offered it to his flock and to his helpers as a compendium of the best and most valuable moments in the history of Christian expression.[28]

Virtually everything Christian was somehow represented in the editions and abridgments that Wesley prepared for his flock, everything except antinomianism. At that he drew the line. That alone was entirely unacceptable to him, and no antinomian writer or sentiment found a place anywhere in his vast publication or ceaseless teaching.[29] He taught Puritanism and latitudinarianism, Jansenism and sentimentalism, monasticism and Anglicanism, mysticism and antislav-

---

[27] Alexander Strachan, *Recollections of the Life and Times of the late Rev. George Lowe* (London, 1848), p. 63.

[28] For a complete list of Wesley's publications, see Baker, *Union Catalogue*. For a list of the authors represented in the Christian Library, see Robert Monk, *John Wesley* (Nashville, Tenn., 1966), pp. 255–62.

[29] For a full account of Wesley's opposition to antinomianism, see Bernard Semmel, *The Methodist Revolution* (New York, 1973), pp. 23–80.

ery argument, but no antinomianism; and he refrained from including in the Christian Library any excerpts even from Luther or Calvin, although they were deeply important to him. Presumably he was afraid that their writings, even if edited carefully, might still yield to the unwary an antinomian construction.

Wesley's objection to antinomianism was plain enough. It held, he said, that Christ had "abolished" the "moral law," and he insisted that this was altogether wrong. What Christ had actually abolished was just the "ritual law of Moses." Right conduct based on faith was still required of all Christians.[30] At Birmingham, in 1746, he met an antinomian, one of the "pillars" of the movement locally, conversed with him, and then recorded the conversation in his Journal, so that "every serious person" might see "the true picture" of what "antinomianism full-grown" really was.

Do you believe you have nothing to do with the law of God?
"I have not; I am not under the law: I live by faith."
Have you, as living by faith, a right to everything in the world?
"I have; all is mine, since Christ is mine."
May you, then, take anything you will anywhere? suppose out of a shop, without the consent or knowledge of the owner?
"I may, if I want it; for it is mine. Only I will not give offense."
Have you also a right to all the women in the world?
"Yes, if they consent."
And is not that a sin?
"Yes, to him that thinks it a sin; but not to those whose *hearts are free*."

This last assertion, that the male believer whose heart was free had a right to any consenting woman, was no doubt especially horrifying to Wesley. "Surely," he said, "these are the first-born children of Satan!"[31]

Minus antinomianism, Wesley's publication was still extraordinarily mixed. It was various in tone, and the authors whom he edited contradicted each other in argument too. At points they also contradicted him, in what he had said or written in his own person, in some one or another of his varying emphases, reformer or parson, anti-Pelagian or neo-Pelagian.[32] To find a single, unifying theological

[30]*Minutes of Conferences*, I: 3–4.
[31]Curnock, 3: 237–38.
[32]For some notice of the contradictions, see Thomas Herbert, *John Wesley as Editor and Author* (Princeton, N.J., 1940), pp. 26–27. In his abridging Wesley had edited

thread running through this mass of edited material is impossible, although many latter-day commentators have tried, wanting to claim Wesley for this or that denominational tradition. Nor is it sufficient to say of Wesley that he was eclectic and ecumenical in his tastes. That is of course true, and it is also true that Wesley was probably as widely read as anybody of his day.

But there is a thread, a pattern, that runs through the Christian Library and all the rest of the written material Wesley gave his flock. The pattern is not theological; it is affective, emotional. Everything that Wesley provided came through him. In every case he rewrote or abridged or pirated or plagiarized. To this general rule there are no exceptions. Not once did Wesley reprint anything by any author without either redoing it or removing the author's name from the title page. Often he did both. Far into the nineteenth century, the Methodists still believed that Wesley had written *The Fool of Quality*, for he had excised from his edition all mention of the real author, Henry Brooke.[33] In his editions of the tracts of the Puritan Thomas Goodwin, of the monk Macarius, of the mystic Mme. Bourignon, Wesley let the authors' names appear, but he made it clear that he had rewritten all of the material, made it the way it should be. In his edition of Samuel Johnson's tract *Taxation No Tyranny*, he revised the prose and removed the author's name as well.

Some of this processing was no doubt practical in an immediate sense. Wesley needed to abridge, because he was providing reading matter for a flock that included many who were unused to reading much. But that need to abridge, however real and pressing, cannot explain why Wesley revised everything by anybody else that he ever republished. His revision of George Herbert, for instance, was more in the nature of a poetic reconstruction than an abridgment.[34] Nor can the need to abridge explain why Wesley sometimes excised the names of the authors of the texts he was republishing.

It is important to note that Wesley stuck to this rewriting, pirating,

out some material that he disliked, but he could never have made The Christian Library or anything else consistent with himself completely.

[33] Wesley had not put his own name to the book. But it came from his press and was distributed through the usual Methodist channels. See T. B. Shepherd, *Methodism and the Literature of the Eighteenth Century* (London, 1940), p. 91.

[34] For an account of Wesley's editing of Herbert, see Helen Vendler, *The Poetry of George Herbert* (Cambridge, Mass., 1975), pp. 121–36.

and plagiarizing even though he got into serious trouble doing so. At least once he was actually sued in the Court of Chancery. Robert Dodsley, the printer who held the copyrights for Young's *Night Thoughts* and the works of Elizabeth Rowe, both authors whom Wesley had plagiarized, moved in 1745 to have a Chancery bill issued against him. To keep the case from coming to trial, Wesley had to pay £50 and promise never to plagiarize those particular authors again.[35] Besides this brush with the law, Wesley had to deal with his opponents, who knew what he was doing, and who attacked him for it continuously. Probably the fiercest of the attacks came when he plagiarized Samuel Johnson's *Taxation No Tyranny* and got accused in the public press of thievery.[36]

Despite the brush with the law, despite the continuous attacks, Wesley kept to his custom of processing everything he republished. He kept to this custom because it served an important purpose. It guaranteed that the reading material the Methodists bought at the society-rooms and from the helpers would always bear his own imprint. It would come from him. Wesley was prepared to give them virtually anything Christian, except antinomianism. But he had to be the source. That the various books he provided conflicted with each other, or with one or another of his own previous statements, mattered to him relatively little.[37] What was important, what was essential, was that the Methodists should continue to look just to him. Like his great evangelical predecessor, Wesley wanted to be "all things to all men."

From everything that Wesley offered the Methodists theologically, as he held their attention fixed just on himself, they selected out what they jointly knew and valued already, Puritanism. That the Methodists were Puritans was clear to their contemporaries, so clear that Samuel Johnson in his great *Dictionary* could define Methodist as

[35] Telford, *Letters*, 2: 27–28.

[36] For a full account of the consequences of this particular plagiarism, see Henry Abelove, "John Wesley's Influence During His Lifetime on the Methodists" (Ph.D. dissertation, Yale University, 1978), pp. 209–20. On one occasion Wesley even claimed to have written a book that his father had written. Telford, *Letters*, 3: 162.

[37] He did make some effort to weed out the contradictions in the Christian Library in preparation for a revised edition. Herbert, *John Wesley*, p. 27.

"one of a new kind of puritans lately arisen."[38] All the rest of the mix that Wesley provided, they ignored. As for the Christian Library, the fifty-volume sampler that he gathered and processed for them, they let it sit unbought on the shelves of the warehouse in London. Of all Wesley's many publishing ventures, the Christian Library was possibly the only one that failed disastrously. By 1783 he had lost about £100 on it and grumbled to his Journal, "Perhaps the next generation may know the value of it."[39]

Their Puritanism was different certainly from that of the preceding era. For they were mostly poor and relatively unlearned, whereas during the sixteenth and seventeenth centuries, many men and women of substance and learning had been Puritans and had contributed largely to setting the agenda of the movement as a whole. To the Methodists, the old Puritan ideal of a learned clergy meant comparatively little. Nor were they especially committed to the old Puritan ideal of cleansing church and nation. After all they typically stood outside the political nation and had very little direct share in national affairs. Under Elizabeth and James I Parliament had always included many Puritans. That was natural, inevitable. For Parliament consisted of a sampling of the propertied, and many of the propertied were Puritans.[40] Under George II and George III Parliament still consisted of a sampling of the propertied, but so few of the propertied were Methodists that from 1738 to 1790 no Methodist sat in Parliament.[41] Only a revolutionary upheaval could have brought the Methodists into close contact with national affairs, as in the 1640's an upheaval had brought the poorer part of the Puritans forward and provided them at once with a voice and an opportunity. But the mid-

---

[38] Noted by John A. Newton, *Methodism and the Puritans* (London, 1964), p. 1.

[39] Frank Baker, "Methodism and Literature in the Eighteenth Century," *Proceedings of the Wesley Historical Society*, 22 (Sept. 1940): 182; Curnock, 4: 48.

[40] It was commonly said at the time of James I's first Parliament that three-quarters of the members were Puritans. See Samuel R. Gardiner, *History of England from the Accession of James I to the Outbreak of the Civil War* (London, 1884), 1: 178. A later authority is willing to say: "Probably a large majority of the House of Commons in 1604–1610 was Puritan in outlook." Wallace Notestein, *The House of Commons, 1604–1610* (New Haven, Conn., 1971), p. 40.

[41] Sir Lewis Namier and John Brooke, eds., *The House of Commons, 1754–1790* (London, 1964), 1: 116; Romney Sedgwick, ed., *The House of Commons, 1715–1754* (London, 1970).

eighteenth century was comparatively stable, at least at the center of the political nation, and the Methodists remained outside.

These old ideals did not entirely disappear. They survived among the Methodists in attenuated form. Wesley built a school for the male children of the helpers, and he ran it in the hope that some at least of the scholars there would want to grow up to be helpers too. It was called Kingswood. Wesley set the curriculum, edited the textbooks himself, and starting in about 1763 asked the Methodists once every year for a contribution to keep the school going. Although poor, they contributed generously, £100 9s. 7d. in 1765, £283 6d. in 1775, £507 12s. in 1785,[42] and to that extent, anyway, still supported the old ideal of the learned clergy. They took no steps together as a group to cleanse church and nation. But the signs and imagery of that old ideal were dear to them. When they wanted to open their first preaching-house in London, they chose to lease the old ruined Foundery, where formerly the army's cannon had been cast. When they outgrew the Foundery and built themselves a chapel, they used as pillars the masts taken from old ships of the line.[43] In the choice of the Foundery, in the use of the masts, they acted out in reduced, or maybe rather imaginative form, the militant, driving public aspiration that had once before brought real cannon and ships into action, overthrown episcopacy, beheaded a king, and founded a new nation.

As they listened to Wesley, they recovered principally three elements of the Puritan heritage they shared: the ideal of a new birth; the ideal of a personal relation of spiritual experience, as an important facet of membership in the group; and the ideal of an imminent apocalypse. But they recovered all three in a changed form, suited to their position and their needs.

What they meant by new birth they explained over and over again, in their diaries, their journals, and their spiritual letters. It was always the same experience but fresh and unique-feeling for each convert. At first the converts-to-be were usually living a mere legal life, relying on good behavior to win God's favor, flattering themselves that they were anyhow less "vile and wicked" than "others."[44] But then they would learn through reading the Bible or maybe hearing a godly

---

[42]*Minutes of Conferences*, 1: 49, 119, 170.
[43]Leslie Church, *The Early Methodist People* (London, 1948), pp. 57, 84.
[44]Robert Dickinson, *Life of the Rev. John Braithwaite* (London, 1825), p. 11.

sermon or maybe conversing with a Christian friend that such good behavior was illusory. In fact each was a sinner in heart and deed, "Guilty of all those Crimes" that he or she had "Disdainfully Lookd on others for."[45] After the conviction of their own sinfulness had sunk in, they would repent and pray God for pardon. This period of conviction and repentance might last a short time. It might also last a long time, say, "two years,"[46] or even more. Along the way the converts-to-be would learn something else, again maybe through reading the Bible or hearing a sermon or conversing with a Christian friend. They would learn that pardon would come only through believing in Christ as Savior, only through "faith."[47] Once they learned that, they would struggle for faith while continuing to repent and pray. Sometimes the struggle might become almost physical, as in the case of the Methodist man who refrained from sleep for five days running, while he begged for faith and forgiveness.[48] Sometimes it would be brief and internal only. But all who sought truly would find what they sought. In an instant, they would believe, Christ would somehow appear "within,"[49] and they would know that they were pardoned. This experience would make for a strange and wonderful moment: one woman might find so much "love" in her "heart" that she could "hardly contain" herself; another might sense suddenly a "Great Calm"; one man might feel so deeply moved as to think that his "heart" was about to be "rent" in "sunder."[50]

Always the pardon, the justification, would come through faith alone. Regardless of Wesley's shifts in emphasis in his own teaching, the Methodists stuck fast to the Reformation doctrine. Once pardoned, the convert would be an entirely new person. As one Methodist woman beautifully explained, "I found myself quite another."[51]

[45]Mary Ramsay to Charles Wesley, June 4, 1740, Methodist Archive.

[46]James Flewitt to Charles Wesley, Nov. 1741, ibid.

[47]Joseph Beaumont, *Memoirs of Mrs. Mary Tatham, Late of Nottingham* (New York, 1839), p. 59.

[48]Richard Burdsall, *Memoirs of the Life of Richard Burdsall* (3d ed., Thetford, 1823), pp. 41–42.

[49]*The Efficacy of Faith in the Atonement of Christ: Exemplified in a Memoir of Mr. William Carvasso, Written by Himself and Edited by His Son* (11th ed.; London, 1847), p. 35.

[50]Sarah Middleton to Charles Wesley, May 25, 1740, Methodist Archive; James Flewitt to Charles Wesley, Nov. 1741, ibid.; Mrs. Plat to Charles Wesley, 1740, ibid.

[51]Mary Ramsay to Charles Wesley, June 4, 1740, ibid.

Remade, reborn by the miracle of grace, converts could go on to amend their ways, confident that if they continued to watch and pray and believe, they could keep down the "power" of "temptation."[52]

This was the Methodist new birth, and it was much like the Puritan new birth, except possibly for one difference. Perhaps ordinarily Puritans would feel themselves pardoned during the course of a godly sermon or immediately in consequence of one. It is less clear that the Methodists depended for their conversion experiences quite so usually or directly on sermons. This difference, if it is a difference, is a matter of nuance, of proportion, and cannot of course be proved. But sermons were less basic in the economy of Methodist than Puritan life. Besides, the helpers were occasionally rather inarticulate. Certainly, some of the Methodists were converted while hearing the word preached,[53] but some and possibly more relatively speaking than among the Puritans would report conversions made elsewhere and incidentally, at work or at home. One Congleton woman, laboring under convictions of her own sinfulness, was standing next to a barn, near some hens. She picked up an egg, hurled it against the barn, and said despairingly, "I shall be damned as sure as that egg is broken." But to her "astonishment," the egg "rebounded from the wall" unbroken, and her "Despair" gave way to "confidence."[54] Another Methodist, a Bristol man, in the course of a walk, suddenly "saw the Lord Jesus standing in the form of a man, holding both his inestimably precious hands upright, and from the palms thereof the blood streaming down." At that moment he was "justified" and never "doubted" again.[55] In everyday scenes and everyday circumstances, the Methodists sometimes made their discovery of grace.

To some Methodists, Wesley's teaching of Perfection was unpalatable. Its novelty puzzled and worried them. As one London woman

[52]Beaumont, p. 63.

[53]See, for instance, Mrs. Plat to Charles Wesley, 1740, Methodist Archive. See Patricia Caldwell, *The Puritan Conversion Narrative* (Cambridge, Eng., 1983), p. 10, for an instance of the centrality of preaching in Puritan conversion.

[54]J. B. Dyson, *History of Wesleyan Methodism in the Congleton Circuit* (London, 1856), pp. 81–82.

[55]Silas Told, *An Account of the Life and Dealings of God With Silas Told, Late Preacher of the Gospel* (London, 1786), p. 107.

wrote to Charles, "I thought the best Christians did sin while they lived here."[56] But Wesley, at least in one of his voices, kept insisting on it anyway. He preached about it often and forcefully. In one sermon, delivered in London, he talked of the difference between justification and Perfection. According to the report of a local Methodist, who heard the sermon, Wesley explained that the two were easily distinguished,

by supposing a professor of each to stand up. Ask the first, have you no pride or anger or desire? He will answer, Yes: I find much of these evils in my heart and at Times they greatly trouble me; but by the grace of God, I can keep them under and desire to press to the prize of my high calling. Ask the other the same questions, and he will answer, No. By the grace of God I find no Remains of any Evil and have likewise the Witness from above that they are all done away and the Change was instantaneous.[57]

Along with his preaching, Wesley conversed about Perfection. A Macclesfield woman, one of those who felt that they had attained it, told him despondently of the Methodists in the local society who disbelieved the claims and testimonies of at least some of the Perfected. He replied encouragingly, warmly: "Well but . . . You and Me, Hetty, do not limit God—and indeed the time is *now* come when a fuller dispensation of the Spirit is given, then has ever been known before."[58]

Just as he encouraged her, so also he stood ready to rebuke anybody who in his hearing questioned Perfection. At a lovefeast he attended, again at Macclesfield, sometime early in the 1780's, several of the Perfected rose one after another and told of their experiences. One "Declared" he had "rec'd Sanctification in a Moment by Simple Faith." Others repeated "the Same precious truths." But then a man spoke up, professing only justification, and saying also that he "own'd he did not experience what he had now heard many profess to do, tho a Methodist 20 years." Instantly Wesley arose and flashed back, "Those who love God with all their Heart must expect most Opposition from professors who have gone on for 20 years in a Lazy old beaten Track and fancy they are wiser than all the world."[59] What the

[56] Joan Webb to Charles Wesley, May 1742, Methodist Archive.
[57] William Briggs to Charles Wesley, Nov. 10, 1762, ibid.
[58] This is of course her record of his words. Hester Roe Rogers journal, ibid.
[59] Ibid.

man at whom this rebuke was aimed must have felt in hearing it cannot be known, can only be guessed. Probably he felt hurt and divided from his brethren, and probably whenever Perfection was much insisted on, by Wesley or by anybody else, some sort of division developed in the society.[60] But what of the Methodists who actually accepted Wesley's teaching on Perfection? How did *they* understand it? Some doubtless understood just exactly what he meant. At least one Methodist who experienced an instantaneous Perfecting (the "promise" was suddenly "applied" to his mind: "Thou art all fair, my love; there is no spot in thee") reported that when he later read Wesley's tract *A Plain Account of Christian Perfection*, he found with "amazement" that what was written there corresponded entirely to his own experience.[61] But some who said they accepted Wesley's teaching can have understood him hardly at all. They knew that they wanted to do what he asked, that they wanted to please him, but knew little more than that. Take, for instance, the strange illogic of the helper who said that he intended to seek for Perfection because he felt "fully convinced" that once he had it he would be both "a better Christian, and a more useful and profitable preacher."[62] Some, finally, understood Wesley's teaching on Perfection in a very special way of their own. They understood him as saying that the Perfected, "dwelling in Love and in God," had "a Heaven below."[63]

For the Methodists who understood Wesley in this way, Perfection was a readily assimilable idea. It was familiar, and it was unthreatening to their plain, shared notions of basic Christian dogma. Perfection was just the old Puritan apocalypse, internalized.[64] It was an instantaneous change that produced "Heaven below," but inside the

---

[60]That is what the evidence seems to show. See, for instance, William Ellis to Charles Wesley, Dec. 23, 1762, Methodist Archive; and Anthony Steele, *History of Methodism in Barnard Castle* (London, 1857), p. 76.

[61]*Efficacy of Faith*, pp. 40–41.

[62]Dickinson, p. 103.

[63]Hester Roe Rogers journal, n.d., Methodist Archive. Another and quite different way of understanding Perfection was discussed in Chap. 5: as a sanction for wives to abstain from sexual relations with their husbands.

[64]See Joy Gilsdorf, "The Puritan Apocalypse" (Ph.D. dissertation, Yale University, 1964). See also, for background, Richard H. Popkin, ed., *Millenarianism and Messianism in English Literature and Thought, 1650–1800* (Leiden, 1988).

believer, rather than in the world at large. Much the biggest local group of the Perfected belonged to the London society, and apparently many of them held to the understanding of Perfection as apocalypse. For in 1763 they drew Wesley's anger down on them by letting their "Heaven below" shift suddenly from a treasure inside to an expectation outside.

What happened was that Wesley gave over a group of the Perfected of London to the charge of one of his ablest helpers. Under the guidance of this helper, who was backed by several able assistants, the group began to develop a rather independent style and outlook. One of the signs of this independence was that their sense of apocalypse spread outward. They came to believe, or some of them did, anyway, that the world was going to end on February 28, and they said so publicly. Shortly after they publicized this prophecy, Wesley effectively forced them out of the Methodist society. He wanted no truck with "enthusiasm," and their imminent millenarian expectation he characterized as "utter absurdity."[65]

To his fellow evangelicals among the clergy, the source of the "rant and madness" among the Londoners was obvious: it was Perfection.[66] This Wesley earnestly denied. He insisted that the "extravagances" of his Perfected followers had no "foundation" in any "doctrine" that he taught, and he said that the Perfection he preached was simply "the loving God with all our heart, soul, and strength, and the loving all men as Christ loved us."[67] But regardless what Wesley taught, or said he taught, apocalypse was what some of his followers learned.

It was important to the Puritans that they know their own hearts and spiritual development. To keep track of themselves and of God's gracious dealings with them was useful as a means of self-testing, as a means of edification, and as a means of demonstrating to their brethren their claim to a place among the elect.[68]

In New England the relation of a conversion experience became

[65]Curnock, 4: 541; 5: 9.

[66]Quoted by Tyerman, *Life and Times*, 2: 463. These words are from a letter from the Rev. William Romaine to the Countess of Huntingdon.

[67]Telford, *Letters*, 4: 206.

[68]See, for instance, William Haller, *The Rise of Puritanism* (New York, 1938), especially pp. 96–97.

actually a formal requirement of admission to the church. Candidates would normally have to appear before the full membership and make an oral relation, maybe fifteen minutes long, of how God's grace had come to them. After they had finished, some questions concerning their relation might be put. If their relation and their answers to the questions were thought satisfactory, they would proceed to make also a statement of creed, and then they would be received as members, as visible saints.[69]

In the Old World, too, the Separating Puritans probably required, if less formally, some "public profession" from a candidate for membership.[70] This requirement of a "public profession" was still in force here and there in the dissenting congregations of the eighteenth century.[71] Among the Methodists no such profession or relation was required for admission. In fact Methodism was entirely open. Anybody might join who, as Wesley liked to say, quoting the New Testament, wanted "to flee from the wrath to come." But once admitted, members were expected to make some kind of public relation of their spiritual experiences at least once every week at a class meeting; again at a band meeting, if they belonged to a band; again at a select-band meeting, if they belonged to a select-band; possibly at the monthly or quarterly lovefeast; and possibly also at the full society meetings, whenever they happened to be scheduled.

One way of characterizing Methodist spirituality would be to say that it was the Puritan relation made continuous. Sermons, after all, were less important to the Methodists than to the Puritans. For the Methodists might hear Wesley only a couple of times a year. As for the helpers, they too appeared only occasionally. But the Methodists could talk about themselves anytime. They could share with one another the developing record of their hopes and fears, faults and successes, doubts and certainties, anxieties and loves. This was what they liked to do; this was what they found "comfortable."[72]

In Wesley's teaching, the Methodists found an opportunity to reappropriate their Puritan heritage, and they reappropriated it in a form pleasing to themselves. Of the old Puritan ideals of the learned

---

[69] Edmund S. Morgan, Jr., *Visible Saints* (New York, 1963), p. 87.
[70] David D. Hall, *The Faithful Shepherd* (Chapel Hill, N.C., 1972), p. 26.
[71] McLachlan, pp. 34–35.
[72] James Chubb diary, Oct. 22, 1778, Methodist Archive.

clergy, of the commitment to the cleansing of church and nation, they needed and took very little. But they regained the Puritan new birth, oriented perhaps away from the pulpit toward the scenes of their everyday life; the Puritan apocalypse, internalized; and the Puritan relation, made continuous, made into an "egotistical sublime."[73]

[73]This phrase is of course Keats's description of Wordsworth's poetry. I use it here to lead up to a point I want to make in passing. It seems to me that to review this account of the spirituality of the Methodist people is to gain a potentially useful perspective on the origins of Romanticism. The discovery of grace at everyday places; the internalization of apocalypse; the privileged and continuous self-exploration and self-expression: these are the basic features of the Methodist appropriation of the Puritan tradition, and they may also have been among the basic features of the poetry that Wordsworth and Coleridge introduced in 1798. For a different view of the connection between Methodism and Romanticism, see Richard E. Brantley, *Wordsworth's Natural Methodism* (New Haven, Conn., 1975).

Chapter Seven

Daily Conduct

Wesley wanted the Methodists to rise early in the morning, to refrain from all the biblically named moral sins, to refrain also from dissipations like play-going and drinking, to submit to authority, and to love each other and everybody else as well.

First of all he wanted them to rise early, at four o'clock without fail. Then they were to attend a prayer-meeting at five o'clock. Every society was supposed to hold such a prayer-meeting every day, summer and winter alike. To Wesley early rising and early prayers were actually the most basic of all Methodist usages. They somehow distinguished the movement, made it what it was. He warned that if "the morning preaching" were ever "given up," Methodism would "degenerate into a mere sect, only distinguished by some opinions and modes of worship."[1] So important were these usages to him that he spoke of them often and insistently, perhaps more insistently than he realized. Once at Sheffield he preached on the text, "Now it is high time to awake out of sleep." His subject apparently was spiritual awakening, but he spoke also of his scheme of early rising. Afterward he received a letter commenting on the sermon from one of his hearers. To Wesley's chagrin all the hearer remembered was the insistence on early rising.[2]

Morally, Wesley's instructions were simple and clear-cut. Every Methodist was supposed to "evidence" his or her "Desire of Salvation" first of all "By doing no Harm." Particularly one was to avoid

[1]Nehemiah Curnock, ed., *The Journal of the Rev. John Wesley, A.M.* (London, 1909–16), 6: 485.
[2]Ibid., 7: 180.

such "Evil" as was most "generally practis'd." In that category Wesley included the "taking of the Name of GOD in vain"; the "profaning of the Day of the LORD"; "fighting, quarelling, brawling"; "uncharitable conversation"; and "usury." All these prohibitions Wesley derived from God's "written Word, the only Rule," the Bible.[3]

To help enforce these biblical prohibitions, Wesley distributed short, cheap pamphlets of advice and warning. One he called *Remember the Sabbath Day*, and it began, peremptorily, "Have you forgotten who spoke these words?" It climaxed tersely, with this direction: "Spend this Day, as thou Hopest to spend that Day which never shall have an end."[4] Another of the little pamphlets was *Swear Not at All*, and like the pamphlet on the observance of the Sabbath it began by drawing attention to the biblical origin of the prohibition. Immediately following the title, *Swear Not at All*, came the words, "Saith the Lord God of Heaven and Earth." Then the reader was asked, again peremptorily, "Hast thou no Knowledge of God?"[5]

Along with the biblical prohibitions Wesley set a general rule against "doing" anything "not for the Glory of GOD."[6] Here the activities forbidden were diversions, self-indulgences, dissipations. During the course of the years Wesley specified which activities he especially blamed. These included dram-taking (drinking spirits), snuff-taking, tea-drinking, theater-going, "the Singing those Songs, or reading those Books, which do not tend to the Knowledge or Love of God," bodily dirtiness, and all "play" whatsoever.[7] Play was for-

[3][John Wesley], *The Nature, Design, and General Rules of the United Societies in London, Bristol, Kingswood, and Newcastle-upon-Tyne* (4th ed.; London, 1744), p. 4, 5, 7. I quote from the edition designated as 4 in Frank Baker, *Union Catalogue of the Publications of John and Charles Wesley* (Durham, N.C., 1966), p. 47.

[4]John Wesley, *Remember the Sabbath Day* (n.p., n.d.), pp. 1–2. I quote from the printing designated as G in Baker, *Union Catalogue*, p. 65.

[5][John Wesley], *Swear Not At All* (n.p., n.d.), p. 1. I quote from the printing designated as A in Baker, *Union Catalogue*, p. 64.

[6]Wesley, *Nature, Design*, p. 7.

[7]*Minutes of the Methodist Conferences* (London, 1862), 1: 53, 58; Curnock, 3: 245–46; Wesley, *Nature, Design*, p. 5; John Telford, ed., *The Letters of the Rev. John Wesley, A.M.* (London, 1931), 4: 279; John Wesley, *A Short Account of the School in Kingswood, near Bristol* (Bristol, 1749), p. 5 (I quote from the printing that Baker, *Union Catalogue*, p. 84, lists first). On some of the forms of play then popular, see Robert Malcolmson, *Popular Recreations in English Society, 1700–1850* (Cambridge, Eng., 1973).

bidden to children as well as adults. On this point Wesley was rigorous and unbending. "He that plays when he is a child," Wesley explained, "will play when he is a Man."[8]

Politically, Wesley insisted in a conventionally tory style on obedience to "authority."[9] As he traveled and preached he sometimes spoke directly of public affairs, almost always defending king and ministers and advising submission. But on at least two occasions he spoke briefly in a rather different key. In the early 1770's, for just a short while, he sided with the Americans against the ministry, and dilated on their injuries and rightful complaints. He also campaigned in Bristol for a pro-American candidate for Parliament.[10] Reading Samuel Johnson's *Taxation No Tyranny* sometime in 1774, he changed his mind, decided that the ministry was right in the quarrel with the Americans, and from then on staunchly defended the government.

His second step out of pattern came in the late 1770's and in 1780. In that period he strongly opposed the ministry's policy of relaxing the penal laws against Roman Catholics and attacked it in the press.[11] Here he was siding with Lord George Gordon's Protestant Association. When riots broke out in London in 1780, encouraged by the association's agitation, Wesley withdrew, spoke disapprovingly of the rioters, and resumed his usual pro-government position.[12] These were perhaps the only two occasions when he moved actively against the government, and both times he reverted to form in short order. He also disapproved of some usages that the government sanctioned, particularly impressment and the slave trade, and he expressed his disapproval freely.[13] But generally he taught submission, insisted on

[8] Wesley, *Short Account*, p. 5.

[9] Wesley, *Nature, Design*, p. 5.

[10] For the story of Wesley's campaign for a pro-American candidate for Parliament, see Henry Abelove, "John Wesley's Influence During His Lifetime on the Methodists" (Ph.D. dissertation, Yale University, 1978), pp. 209–20.

[11] Telford, *Letters*, 6, 370–73.

[12] See *The Protestant Association: Written in the Midst of the Tumults* (London, 1781). Probably by John or Charles Wesley.

[13] Curnock, 2: 245. For a discussion of Wesley's views on slavery, see David Brion Davis, *The Problem of Slavery in Western Culture* (Ithaca, N.Y., 1966), pp. 382–89; and Bernard Semmel, *The Methodist Revolution* (New York, 1973), especially pp. 94–96.

obedience to the law, even the law against smuggling, and after every meal he ate, as he traveled from one Methodist home to another, he asked for a blessing on the king.[14]

Along with his demand that the Methodists rise and pray early, refrain from the biblically named moral sins, refrain also from dissipations, and submit to authority, Wesley demanded that they do good, too. He told them to be "merciful after their power," as they might have "opportunity," and "as far" as "possible," to "all Men." But he enjoined them especially to care for "them that are of the Household of Faith, or groaning so to be: Employing them preferably to others, buying one of another, helping each other in Business."[15]

These, then, were Wesley's rules for everyday living. To the first of the rules, the rule requiring them to rise at four and pray at five o'clock, the Methodists responded coldly. If Wesley himself was the scheduled preacher, then they might attend. They might even come early. Once in Cornwall, a "company of tinners" arrived sometime between three and four and woke him up, singing hymns outside the house where he was staying.[16] But Wesley's personal presence made for a very special occasion. In ordinary times only a few of the faithful came—a woman, for instance, so anxious that she "frequently would not go to bed all night, lest she should miss the morning preaching," or a man so determinedly obedient that he choked down his own skepticism about early rising, a rule, he remarked, nowhere "expressly commanded" in the Scripture, and duly attended at five, with "joy and satisfaction."[17] These early risers were the exception. No matter how firmly Wesley insisted, the rule was generally ignored. As he traveled, he found that the early service had been altogether discontinued in Dublin as of 1758; in Lisburn as of 1765; in Londonderry as of 1769; and in Ambleside as of 1770. Even in a city as big as Bristol, with an old and established Methodist community, the attendance in the late 1780's was about five to twelve people. At Nor-

[14]Curnock, 8: 143. On his stance toward smuggling, see *Minutes of Conferences*, 1: 74.
[15]Wesley, *Nature, Design*, pp. 5–6.
[16]Curnock, 3: 94. For another such incident, see ibid., 4: 114.
[17]Ibid., 3: 162–63; 4: 205.

wich, in roughly the same period, the congregation consisted sometimes of just three, one of whom was the helper's wife. When reproached about failing to attend, the poorer members of the
Norwich society explained that their work started commonly at eight
o'clock. If they were to rise at four, they would have to heat their cot-
tages for an extra couple of hours every day, and they could not afford
to do so.[18] Shortly after Wesley died the morning service was abolished even in London, his home society.[19]

As for Wesley's injunction against the biblically named moral sins,
this the Methodists accepted wholeheartedly. By forbidding the
breaking of the Sabbath and swearing and fighting, Wesley was after
all reminding them of what they already knew and believed, and of
course helping them recover it, too. They had a beautifully appropriate name for such sins; they called them "known" sins.[20] Of course
they sometimes committed "known" sins. To suppose otherwise
would be naïve. They broke the Sabbath—or swore—or "kept a
married woman company"—or attempted the rape of a ten-year-old
child—or turned highwayman—or committed suicide—or ex-
torted £120—or stole.[21] But as a united group they stuck to their familiar and received understanding that these deeds that Wesley described as sins were in fact sins; they reprobated them, and they at
least wanted to avoid them.

Wesley's injunction against dissipations, diversions, and self-
indulgences they received in a different spirit. Here their response
was mixed. Some of what he condemned, they condemned too, and
perhaps even more strongly than he. But some of what he con-

[18]Ibid., 4: 258; 5: 113, 313, 361; 7: 248; Luke Tyerman, *The Life and Times of the Rev. John Wesley, A.M.* (London, 1870–72), 3: 466.

[19]Curnock, 6: 485.

[20]Eliza Weaver Bradburn, *Memoirs of the Late Rev. Samuel Bradburn* (London, 1816), p. 59.

[21]James Chubb diary, March 23, 1779, Methodist Archive (on "kept a married woman"); ibid., Feb. 21, 1783 (on attempted rape); John S. Pawlyn, *Bristol Methodism in John Wesley's Day* (Bristol, 1877), p. 24 (on becoming a highwayman); George J. Stevenson, *City Road Chapel, London, and Its Associations* (London, n.d.), p. 48 (on suicide); L. Grainger to Joseph Benson, Sept. 2, 1790, Methodist Archive (on ex-tortion); Henry(?) Goodfellow journal, May 12, 1786, Methodist Archive (on steal-ing).

demned they jointly valued, and they persisted in valuing it, regardless of what he said. Perhaps the least successful of his condemnations was the move he made against tea-drinking. First he gave it up himself. Then, in 1746, he urged the rest of the Methodists to do so too. According to his own observation, about one hundred of the London society followed his lead, at least for a time. But the campaign nevertheless plainly failed, and twelve years afterward Wesley himself went back to tea-drinking.[22]

How successful Wesley was in discouraging snuff-taking and dram-taking among the mass of Methodists is hard to say. In all probability he was relatively unsuccessful. For he encountered persistent difficulty in discouraging these habits even among the helpers whom he could fire at will.[23] As for his efforts to discourage bodily dirtiness, here again the record is obscure. But the scant evidence that may now be found suggests that in some regions his instruction on this point was firmly resisted. It was felt as a foreign imposition, and it was resented. Once on the Isle of Jersey, sometime in the late 1780's, the wife of a helper approached one of the local women, "whose children appeared never to have had their faces washed, or their hair combed." Then the helper's wife, "placing the subject in the least objectionable form" possible, asked, " 'Do you think your children are as orderly as they might be?' " To which the local woman answered, " 'Indeed they are.' " Determined to press on, the helper's wife then asked, " 'Would it not be better to wash them?' " To which the return came fast and clear and relevant: " 'O! away with your English pride.' " Still persevering, the helper's wife invoked Wesley, knowing that the local woman "entertained great respect" for him. " 'Does not Mr. Wesley say,—that cleanliness is next to godliness?' " Whereupon the local woman concluded the exchange, saying, " 'Thank God, that is not written in my Bible.' "[24]

On still another matter the Methodists resisted Wesley's rule against indulgences. Contrary to his express prohibition, they let their children play. He told them again and again how children ought really to be raised—awakened of course at four; fed "milk-porridge

[22]Tyerman, *Life and Times*, 1: 523. He went back at the urging of his doctor.
[23]*Minutes of Conferences*, 1: 136.
[24]James Everett, *Adam Clarke Portrayed* (London, 1843), 1: 221–22.

and water gruel, by turns," at supper, meat or vegetables at dinner; employed continuously throughout the day in study, work, meditation, or prayer; put to bed at eight; and never, never, permitted to play.[25] But regardless of how intensely he spoke, there were always some prepared to answer back with "that poor, lame miserable shift, 'Oh, he has no children of his own!' "[26] Once at Manchester, after he had yet again heard "that very silly answer, 'Oh he has no children of his own,' " Wesley put an indignant counterreply into his Journal: " 'Neither had St. Paul, nor (that we know) any of the apostles. What then? Were they, therefore, unable to instruct parents?' "[27]

This invocation of the apostles apparently failed of effect, too. For even at Kingswood, his own school, which he directed personally, Wesley was unable to secure the observance of his rule. He could visit at Kingswood only occasionally. Most of the time he was either itinerating or staying at his lodgings in London. So he was obliged to leave the day-to-day administration of affairs there in the hands of others: hence, the problem. Almost every time he stopped to inquire, he found that his rule was "habitually neglected."[28] He would then reassert the rule, give orders, directions, instructions, but all to no avail. Four years later, back on another visit, he would have to record in his Journal, "I endeavored once more to bring Kingswood school into order."[29] Thirteen years after that: "I rode over to Kingswood, and, having told my whole mind to the masters and servants, spoke to the children in a far stronger manner than ever I did before. I will kill or cure: I will have one or the other—a Christian school, or none at all."[30] And fifteen years after *that*: "Surely Satan has a particular spite at this school! What trouble has it cost me for above these thirty years! I can *plan*, but who will *execute*?"[31]

[25]Wesley, *Short Account*, p. 4.

[26]Curnock, 5: 189.

[27]Ibid., p. 253. In their approval of play for their children, Methodists were probably typical of their English contemporaries. See J. H. Plumb, "The New World of Children," in Neil McKendrick, John Brewer, and J. H. Plumb, eds., *The Birth of a Consumer Society* (London, 1983), pp. 286–315. See also Thomas Laqueur, *Religion and Respectability* (New Haven, Conn., 1976), pp. 9–15.

[28]Curnock, 3: 422.

[29]Ibid., 4: 80.

[30]Ibid., 5: 159.

[31]Ibid., 6: 334.

It was only in 1784, when Wesley was eighty-one and too old obviously to know what exactly was going on, that he could finally say of Kingswood, with much satisfaction, "At length the rules of the house are punctually observed."[32]

All the time that he was blaming Kingswood and trying to bring it under rule, he was upholding as an example of what a school should really be the school that some of his closest women followers were running for orphan girls at Leytonstone. Here, at Leytonstone, Wesley found "a truly Christian family." It was "what that at Kingswood school should be, and would, if it had such governors."[33]

But even at Leytonstone Wesley's rule was not wholly and perfectly observed. At that best of all possible schools, the girls were in fact awakened only at "half past six"—during the "winter," anyway. Their breakfast was as it was supposed to be: it was "either milk-porage—watergrule or Rise milk." Supper, too, was much as Wesley required: "Bread butter or apples and bread." But twice during the daily round of frugal meals, prayer, study, reading, and meditation, the girls were permitted to play. This Wesley did not know. For the custom of the house was: "we never use ye term play." That much they were willing to do to humor him. They dropped the use of the "term." Nevertheless, just before breakfast, the girls were permitted to "Go into ye Garden," and again, just before dinner, to "run in ye Garden or Swing."[34]

So the Methodists were well able to resist such of Wesley's demands as they jointly disapproved. If what he was telling them to relinquish was something they liked, and found no value in relinquishing, as, for instance, tea or drams or snuff, they tended to continue using it, despite what he said. If the prohibition he was trying to impose was experienced as overbearing or culturally threatening, as for some the prohibition against dirtiness was, they probably tended to ignore it, again despite what he said. If the prohibition made no sense to them at all, like the prohibition on children's play, they rejected it outright, and either told him that he was talking from a position of ignorance or humored him. It may be surprising, then,

[32] Ibid., p. 482.
[33] Ibid., 5: 152.
[34] Elizabeth Ritchie, "An Account of the Rise and Progress of the Work of God in Latonstone," 1763, Methodist Archive.

to find that they took his rule against one particular sort of dissipation entirely to heart. When he told them, as *adults*, to avoid play, they accepted what he said as right, and more enthusiastically perhaps than he had intended.

There can be no doubt: the Methodists rejected all forms of adult play. They frowned on dancing, on football, on card-playing (one Methodist woman burned her brother's cards, to help keep him from falling), and above all, on theater.[35] Their feelings against theater especially were unvaryingly negative, and they recalled with horror the play-going they had done formerly in their pre-conversion days. As one woman said, "insted of the church, the play-house was my greatest delight; thus I sought death, in the error of my way."[36] Wesley seldom made a point of preaching against the theater, and the vehemence of the Methodists' hostility may have surprised him. His own sympathies were wide enough to include Shakespeare anyway. In his travels he often took his copy along with him, read it in his spare moments, and made annotations in the margins. After his death one of the helpers found it, annotations and all.[37]

Why should the Methodists have accepted Wesley's prohibition on adult play so wholeheartedly? One of the reasons certainly was that such prohibitions were religiously traditional. But there may have been another reason too. It will be recalled that the basic form of Methodist piety was self-expression. No doubt this self-expression was complicated by self-scrutiny, self-criticism, and even self-abasement, but self-expression was still what it essentially was. For this the Methodists met in classes, in bands, in select-bands, at love-feasts, and in society. At each sort of gathering they took turns talk-

---

[35] John Crook diary, Oct. 17, 1775, Methodist Archive; Richard Burdsall, *Memoirs of the Life of Richard Burdsall* (3d ed.; Thetford, 1823), p. 1; Thomas Percival Bunting, *Life of Jabez Bunting, D.D.* (London, 1859), 1: 8–9; Mary Ramsay to Charles Wesley, June 4, 1740, Methodist Archive. Note also the account of the woman who kept a bookseller's shop and after converting removed all the plays and novels from the shelves. G. H. B. Judge, *Origins and Progress of Wesleyan Methodism in Cheltenham and District* (Cheltenham, 1912), p. 8.

[36] Martha Jones to Charles Wesley, June 1, 1740, Methodist Archive.

[37] T. B. Shepherd, *Methodism and the Literature of the Eighteenth Century* (London, 1940), p. 191. Whitefield, however, did preach often against the theater. Ibid., pp. 192–99.

ing of their experiences and feelings. They told how Satan had tempted them, how God had helped them. They told of what they had just finished doing, of what they were hesitating to do, of what they definitely intended to do. They told of their griefs and hopes, their failures and successes. As each one spoke the others listened, often eagerly, appreciatively. But the others would want to have their turns too, and if the speaker spoke too long, they would grow impatient or resentful. One Methodist, a Duddon Heath man, was considered an offender in this respect. He was virtuous and upright but went to "excess" in "religious exercises." What he had to say he would cast in the form of a prayer, and "when he got his heart warm, he would continue his prayer for 15 or 20 minutes; and thereby prevented others from exercising their talents."[38] Then, too, a speaker might be inarticulate, barely able to hold his own in the exchange. Even so the group might find his words memorable and touching. An Alpraham man, when asked to speak at a lovefeast, could say only this much: "God hath been very good to me, a poor sorry dog as I am."[39] Yet he, too, made an impression. Some speakers, finally, might be shy, particularly if they happened to be new to the group or young. A shy youngster might be given a "Form" to stand on so that he could "be heard." If he then felt "so Confused he c'd not say all he intended," he might afterward be told "many things" to "encourage" him.[40]

Perhaps the Methodists disapproved of adult play, and especially theater, because they had an ongoing theater of their own, which they liked better than the one that dramatists provided. In their theater they were the stars as well as the audience. Their lines were the lines that were remembered and commented upon afterward. Their concerns were the subject of the play, and furthermore they needed to make no rare and hard effort of sensibility to grasp what was happening around them. For the words were familiar, even if heightened, and the others present were just their usual companions, even if especially excited for the occasion.

[38] J. Janion, *Some Account of the Introduction of Methodism into the City, and Some Parts, of the County, of Chester* (Chester, 1833), pp. 94–95.
[39] Ibid., pp. 20–21.
[40] Hester Roe Rogers journal, Methodist Archive.

At some level of mind the Methodists actually knew that they were making a theater of their own. For they sometimes chose to rent old, disused theater buildings to serve as their preaching-houses. They rented theaters at Rochdale, at London, at Newbury, at Wigan, at Sheerness, and at Birmingham.[41] Besides, they arranged for admission to their lovefeasts and society meetings by means of what they called "tickets." These tickets were issued and distributed to all members in good standing four times a year. A current ticket was readily distinguishable. It would be dated, and it would have printed on it some particular text of Scripture. Anybody who came to a society meeting or lovefeast and presented the doorkeeper with an out-of-date ticket would be denied admission.[42]

If the Methodists, then, were making a theater of their own among themselves, they might easily have felt impelled to a hostile view of ordinary theater and ordinary play. For these ordinary forms were similar to what they were making. Yet they wanted to think of what they were making as special, uniquely favored, high. So the all-too-obvious similarity might be threatening enough to evoke fear and anger. Wesley, whose position was far outside the circle of their continuous interpersonal exchanges, would have been relatively detached from the feelings that moved them, and perhaps would never have realized why this one alone of all his prohibitions against dissipation should have been embraced so readily.[43]

As for Wesley's teaching of submission to "authority," that won certainly some measure of acceptance, just as the teaching on early rising had. Here and there Methodists felt as fervently attached to the throne as even Wesley could have wished. As one Methodist man confided loyally to his diary, "[I] have been much stirred up to pray for the King, on hearing that the Fr. and Spsh had took Gibr; had

[41] In fact at Birmingham they rented two different theaters. George Dolbey, *Architectural Expression of Methodism*, p. 30; Curnock, 5: 254, 335, 349.

[42] Frank Baker, "The People Called Methodists—3. Polity," in Rupert Davies and Gordon Rupp, eds., *A History of the Methodist Church in Great Britain* (London, 1965), 1: 224. See also Jean-Christophe Agnew's observations on the revival of what he calls a "theatrical perspective" among the literate classes in eighteenth-century England, in *Worlds Apart* (Cambridge, Eng., 1986), especially pp. 159–60.

[43] In thinking about the Methodists' hostility to adult play and especially theater, I have been aided by Jonas Barish, "Exhibitionism and the Anti-theatrical Prejudice," *Journal of English Literary History*, 36 (March 1969): 1–29.

great confidence for him, that God would preserve him from the fury of his enemies."[44] Another was "pleased" to have the opportunity "to see the royal brothers together" and told a correspondent, "I think we ought to pray for them."[45] But prayers for royalty had to be composed very carefully. One of the helpers erred by praying publicly for the king in such a way as to imply that he was a sinner. As a result, some of the members of the Leeds society, eager echoers of Wesley's royalism, drew up a petition asking that this helper, who was scheduled to preach in their round in the year ensuing, be reassigned elsewhere. According to the helper's account of the matter, the petitioners argued that his prayer had been "calculated to lower royalty in the estimation of the people," and that his "principles" were obviously "dangerously democratic."[46]

Despite these occasional echoes of Wesley's toryism among the Methodists, the fact remains that he never on the whole succeeded in persuading them to obey the laws that they disliked, such as those against smuggling and the buying of smuggled goods. As late as 1802 a helper at Lizard, while walking by the seaside, "saw a smuggler land his goods," and "in consequence of this" landing, found "very few hearers" at the evening preaching.[47]

Besides, the times that Wesley got the warmest public reactions to his politics that he ever succeeded in getting were the very times when he momentarily abandoned his usual pro-government stance and went into active opposition. When, in 1774, he campaigned in Bristol for a radical, pro-American candidate for Parliament, the Methodist voters of Bristol followed his lead willingly, voted overwhelmingly for the radical, and helped significantly in getting him elected.[48] And when, in the late 1770's, Wesley opposed the ministry's policy of relaxing the penal laws against Catholics, the Protestant Association (many of whose members were Methodists) gave him a public vote

---

[44]William Holder diary, April 20, 1770, Methodist Archive.

[45]Samuel Dunn, *Memoirs of Mr. Tho. Tatham and of Wesleyan Methodism in Nottingham* (London, 1847), p. 51.

[46]Everett, *Adam Clarke Portrayed*, 1: 231–32.

[47]Quoted by Leslie Church, *The Early Methodist People* (London, 1948), p. 195.

[48]See Abelove, "John Wesley's Influence," pp. 209–20, for an account of the incident. For background, see John Brewer, *Party Ideology and Popular Politics at the Accession of George III* (Cambridge, Eng., 1976).

of thanks.[49] It may be that Wesley made the most powerful impact on the Methodists when he advocated antigovernment views that they shared anyway.

Typically, the Methodists tended to observe Wesley's rule that they love each other and help each other in business. This rule was easily acceptable on account of the strong sense of union among them. They bought from each other, loaned to each other, and left legacies to each other, as their means allowed. It is true that occasionally enmities erupted in the close-knit little societies, and pettinesses were indulged. One of the helpers even described his Methodist brethren as on the whole "unfit for familiar friendship."[50] But most of the Methodists thought differently; they valued their fellowship, sometimes so much so, that they asked that when they died, their membership tickets be buried with them.[51]

Their difficulty came in observing the latter part of Wesley's rule, that they love outsiders too. This much they certainly did: they gave money to outsiders. Both in London and in Bristol, they established charitable organizations to care for the non-Methodist needy, and they called the organizations "The Stranger's Friend Society."[52] But their generosity seldom resulted in anything more than money or maybe spiritual advice. So strong was their sense of union with one another that no outsiders were really tolerable to them, unless of course the outsiders wanted to join. One Methodist, a Sheffield man, provides an account of how the reaction to an outsider would go. It is an unusual account in being especially full and articulate, but the reaction it describes may be taken as typical. He says that once, when "a strange family" had moved into the neighborhood, he went to call on them. He told them, "after some introductory remarks," that he was a Methodist, that he "feared God," and "had lately begun to inquire the way to heaven." He added that he and his family wished them well and would be glad to do them any feasible "office of kindness," but on one condition only: that they turned out to be "likeminded with reference to the salvation of their souls." If they were

---

[49] It was voted in February 1780. See Eugene Black, *The Association* (Cambridge, Mass., 1963), pp. 157–58.

[50] Dunn, p. 18.

[51] Thomas Shaw, *A History of Cornish Methodism* (Truro, 1967), p. 49.

[52] Curnock, 7: 49; Telford, *Letters*, 7: 308.

not, then he could have no "familiarity or acquaintance with them," because "the friendship of the world was enmity against God."[53]

In short, the Methodists discriminated among the rules for daily conduct that Wesley set for them, and took what they could turn to their own purposes. What they disliked, or what was beyond their reach, they rejected.

[53]*Life of Henry Longden, Minister of the Gospel, Compiled from His Memoirs, Diary, Letters, and Other Authentic Documents* (New York, 1837), p. 31. For some further instances of Methodist reaction to outsiders, see Alexander Strachan, *Recollections of the Life and Times of the late Rev. George Lowe* (London, 1848), pp. 58–59; and Basil Cozzens-Hardy, ed., *Diary of Sylas Neville* (Oxford, 1950), p. 145.

Chapter Eight

The Succession

Wesley really wanted nobody to succeed him. His position as leader of the Methodists was a monopoly while he lived, and he intended it to remain so even after he died.

It is true that he made an offer of the succession to his friend and clerical sympathizer John Fletcher, the vicar of Madeley. From Wesley's point of view Fletcher had many of the qualities that the job demanded. First, he had a "striking person." Then, too, he had "good breeding" and a "winning address." Along with these advantages he had a rich "flow of fancy," a strong "understanding," a great "treasure of learning," and "above all," a "deep and constant communion with the Father and with the Son, Jesus Christ."[1] Nobody else, as Wesley saw the matter, was nearly so well qualified for the succession, and in January 1773 he sent Fletcher a letter declaring, "Thou art the man!"[2]

But Wesley can hardly have believed that the offer would be accepted. Fletcher was foreign-born, Swiss. He had first arrived in England and begun to learn the language when he was already twenty-three years old. To the mass of the Methodists he was still a foreigner and would be a foreigner as long as he lived; he could never have led them successfully. Besides, he was sickly, or maybe just anxious about his health. As he told a friend of his: "My throat is not formed for the labours of preaching. When I have preached three or four times together, it inflames and fills up; and the efforts, which I am then

[1] Quoted by Luke Tyerman, *Wesley's Designated Successor* (New York, 1883), p. 265.
[2] John Telford, ed., *The Letters of the Rev. John Wesley, A.M.* (London, 1931), 6: 11.

obliged to make, heat my blood."[3] In fact Fletcher spent three of the ten years that followed his getting the offer of the succession in the south of Europe, just taking care of himself. His reply to Wesley's letter was the firm no that Wesley must have expected and counted on.[4]

In 1784, at the age of eighty-one, Wesley made another kind of offer of the succession. If before, in the gesture to Fletcher, he had offered the position to somebody who was nearly his peer but bound to refuse, this time he offered it to those who were glad to accept but in no way his peers—his helpers, or rather some of them. What he did was to file in the Court of Chancery a deed stipulating that the powers he enjoyed in Methodism during his lifetime were to be assumed after his death by a group of 100 of the helpers, whose names he subjoined.[5] This group was to meet yearly, call itself the "Conference," and co-opt new members from the full body of helpers whenever necessary. It was also to elect a president, who was to conduct the yearly meeting and exercise such further authority as the conference might choose to give him. At the meeting the president would have two votes, all ninety-nine other members would have one vote each, and the decison on any controverted point would be as majority ruled.[6]

When Wesley filed this deed in Chancery, there were 188 helpers all together. So a substantial number were excluded from the conference. They were free to remain as helpers, and Wesley urged the conference to remember always to treat the excluded brethren fairly. Still, some of the excluded took offense and broke away from Methodism.[7] As for the helpers named in the deed, they willingly accepted Wesley's offer of the succession.

Wesley did more for the helpers than give them, or rather some of

[3] Tyerman, *Wesley's Successor*, p. 270.
[4] Ibid., pp. 263–64. Fletcher, in his letter of refusal, made clear that he thought Charles would be the proper choice.
[5] Actually Wesley named only 96 helpers. He named also two clerical sympathizers, his brother Charles, and himself. He named himself because the group was to begin to exist immediately, even though it would come to full power only after his death.
[6] For the text of the deed, see Nehemiah Curnock, *The Journal of the Rev. John Wesley, A.M.* (London, 1909–16), 8: 335–41.
[7] Frank Baker, *John Wesley and the Church of England* (Nashville, Tenn., 1970), pp. 228–33.

them, the succession. He gave them something else as well, something that they had long wanted and that he had long withheld, something that would provide them with a standing as necessary for their work after his death as any legal rights a deed might establish. About six months after he filed the deed, he began to ordain them.

Previously, Wesley had discouraged the helpers from seeking ordination. He had admitted that a sizable minority of them were fully able to find some bishop willing to ordain them. In 1769 he estimated that about one-fourth of the helpers could get ordained if they wished and then procure preferment in the church.[8] But Wesley had wanted them to stay as they were, wanted them to be helpers rather than clergymen and gentlemen.

That had been his basic attitude, and he had urged it on them strongly and almost uniformly. Some exceptions had been permitted. When helpers had been sent outside the British Isles, he had occasionally agreed to their applying to a bishop for ordination.[9] He had also maintained in his employ in England a handful of regularly ordained clergymen. These men he paid £60–£80 a year, stationed in Bristol and London, and used chiefly to assist in serving communion to the big Methodist congregations there. They were in effect his curates. Once and maybe only once, he had encouraged a helper who aspired to one of these big-city posts. He had actually recommended the helper for ordination.[10] But Wesley may possibly have felt ambivalent about making the recommendation. For he did not refer the man to some English bishop, who could have conferred orders that would have been generally recognized as valid. Instead Wesley referred him to an impoverished stranger, who spoke no English, called himself by the name Erasmus, and claimed to be the Bishop of Arcadia in the Greek Orthodox church.[11] Erasmus, so-called, ordained the helper, but no Church of England clergyman besides Wesley would acknowledge the ordination. The helper later got the Bishop of London to reordain him and left the Methodists.[12]

[8]*Minutes of the Methodist Conferences* (London, 1862), 1: 88.

[9]Baker, *John Wesley and the Church*, p. 259.

[10]I say maybe only once because Wesley may possibly have done so twice. At any rate he claimed, in a letter of self-justification, to have recommended a helper to somebody who in turn recommended him to a bishop for ordination. See Telford, *Letters*, 4: 209.

[11]Ibid., p. 289.

[12]Charles Atmore, *The Methodist Memorial* (Bristol, 1801), p. 224.

In 1784, after filing the deed, Wesley changed his attitude about the desirability of ordination for the helpers, and he began to ordain them with his own hands. At first he ordained only those about to set out for America. Then he ordained some he was sending to Scotland, and finally in 1788 and 1789 he ordained some who were assigned to preaching rounds in England. All in all he ordained twenty-seven as presbyters and two as superintendents, and in doing so, he completed the job of securing a succession.[13]

But the succession he secured by his Chancery deed and his or-dinations was of a peculiar sort. His successors were necessarily weaker than he had been as the leader of Methodism, and they could never really replace him. First of all, the succession consisted of help-ers, whom he had thoroughly subordinated in the eyes of the flock. Second, they had been chosen entirely by him. Some he had included in the conference, others he had excluded. Third, they were required to conduct business democratically, by vote, and they were a big group. No member, not even the president, who had two votes, would ever be easily able to assert himself absolutely, as Wesley had. And although Wesley had at last encouraged the helpers in their drive for ordination, he had ordained them himself. No churchly rule justified him in doing so. Certainly none justified him in making su-perintendents. Ordination was supposed to be the prerogative of bishops only, and Wesley never succeeded in developing a coherent theological rationale to cover what he had done.[14] It made no sense theologically, but it made good sense emotionally. By laying his own hands on the helpers, Wesley accomplished just what he wished: he made them at once independent enough to continue the work and dependent on him forever.

Wesley took one final step to make sure that the succession he was providing would never really replace him. In 1789 he drew his last will and testament. By that will he left to each of the helpers an eight-volume edition of his sermons; to the Kingswood School, in trust, the furnishings of his Kingswood houses; to the helpers collectively, in trust, his personal library, deposited in his various studies throughout the British Isles. But one thing he left to nobody. Of all his personal possessions, the most regal and also the most familiar to the flock was

[13] Baker, *John Wesley and the Church*, pp. 280–82.
[14] See ibid., p. 269.

his carriage with the custom-fitted bookshelves inside. For many years he had made most of his triumphant progresses through the kingdom riding in that carriage. No one was to take his place there. Wesley gave explicit instructions in the will that the carriage and horses were to be sold.[15]

So Wesley's provision of a succession was no Lear-like act of abandon. He kept back far more than he handed on, and he ensured that even after his death he would remain uniquely and powerfully the leader of Methodism.

During these last years, while he was providing for the succession, Wesley thought, as he had often done before, about the special features of the revival that he headed. Again, the feature that he particularly noticed was the continuousness of Methodism. In a letter he wrote to one of the helpers in 1786, he returned once again to the comparison he liked to make between his revival and the Great Awakening in New England:

It is indeed a matter of joy that our Lord is still carrying on His work throughout Great Britain and Ireland. In the time of Dr. Jonathan Edwards there were several gracious showers in New England, but there were large intermissions between one and another; whereas with us there has been no intermission at all for seven-and-forty years, but the work of God has been continually increasing.[16]

No intermission. Continually increasing. These were Wesley's terms, and they were accurate. To make the revival continuous, he had led it very much in his own way. He had contrived to get followers who could be held, and he had held them fast.

In planning to keep the leadership of Methodism even after his death, Wesley may have meant to do more than just gratify his vanity. He may have meant to enable Methodism as a revival movement to continue always. If it had already lasted so long because led by a single, seductive, and monopolizing leader, then maybe it would last indefinitely if the leader remained the leader, if his successors were necessarily weak and subordinate by comparison.

Wesley may have had yet another purpose in remaining as the

---

[15] His last will is conveniently printed in Curnock, 8: 342–44.
[16] Telford, *Letters*, 7: 352.

leader of Methodism, in handing on to his successors only a shadow of his own authority. He may have meant to try to set the Methodist people free. To some considerable extent they had of course been free from the start. Their union with one another, developing paradoxically as a result of the strength of his leadership, had always enabled them to modify his demands to suit their own wants and needs. But Wesley may possibly have wanted to let them go free altogether. He may possibly have wanted to leave them just in each other's keeping.

They arranged for the funeral as they thought he would have liked. In one last act of anxious compliance, they scheduled it at five in the morning. As the clergyman, a longtime sympathizer and employee of Wesley's, read aloud from the prayerbook, the congregation wept silently. But when he came to the point where the prayerbook's words were, "Our dear departed brother," he varied his voice feelingly and said instead, "Our dear departed father." At that the congregation burst into loud sobbing.[17] The seduction, the romance, and the resistance were all done.

[17]Henry Moore, *The Life of the Rev. John Wesley, A.M.* (New York, 1824–26), 2: 232.

BIBLIOGRAPHY

Bibliography

This bibliography has two purposes: first, to mention a few authors who have been especially important to my work, more so than the footnotes might indicate; second, to provide a list of some of the manuscript sources I have consulted and of the books, articles, magazines, and theses I have cited.

First of all I want to name E. P. Thompson, *The Making of the English Working Class*. It was this masterpiece that first sparked my interest in the subject. Thompson deals mostly with the Methodism of the period following Wesley's death (the book concentrates on 1780–1820), but reading about that made me curious about what had gone before. Besides, Thompson does say a little about the earlier Methodism, the Methodism of the period of Wesley's lifetime, and that little left me unpersuaded. He writes of that Methodism as though it were something entirely foreign to England's plebeians, something just imposed on them. It seemed to me unlikely that they would have valued it as they did if they had not found in it the means to fulfill needs and purposes of their own.

How they found the means to do so I learned from studying the records they left behind and from reading Freud, especially his *Group Psychology and the Analysis of the Ego*. Freud argues there that when a group of people puts "one and the same object in the place of their ego ideal," they then identify themselves "with one another in their ego." This identification has, as he says, "significance" for the "intellectual life." He chooses to leave "on one side" the discussion of that significance, and I like to think that I may have picked up the discussion where he left off.

In reading Freud I have used lenses ground by Lacan, especially his *Four Fundamental Concepts of Psychoanalysis*. It is not that I have deployed his theoretical formulations in my work. Nothing of the "There is something of one" appears here. It is rather that I have tried to learn from him to see Freud free and clear of the ideological positions (moralism, medical modeling) long promoted by American ego psychology.

Foucault's books on the history of sexuality (*The History of Sexuality*, *The Use of Pleasure*, *The Care of the Self*) have encouraged me to believe that the story of how human sexualities have been made may yet be told.

I have relied continuously on Frank Baker's *Union Catalogue of the Publications of John and Charles Wesley*, Nehemiah Curnock's edition of Wesley's Journal, and John Telford's edition of Wesley's letters. A new edition of Wesley is now under way. Oxford University Press has published five volumes and Abingdon Press six. But the volumes so far published cover only a part of Wesley's total literary production, and I have continued to cite earlier editions, correcting errors whenever I found them.

Manuscripts

All of the collections listed are housed in the Methodist Archive, John Rylands University Library, Manchester, England, unless otherwise noted.

Samuel Bardsley Papers
James Barritt Papers (transcript)
John Bennet Papers
James Chubb Papers
John Crook Papers
Henry(?) Goodfellow Papers
(?) Hodgson Papers
William Holder Papers
Thomas Illingworth Papers (transcript) in the possession of the Rev. Dr. Frank Baker, on deposit in the Duke University Divinity School Library, Durham, N.C.
Kingswood Society Membership List for 1757, Pierpont Morgan Library, New York
Letters to Charles Wesley
Miscellaneous Letters
George Park Papers, Beinecke Library, Yale University, New Haven, Conn.
Frances Pawson Papers
John Pawson Papers
Elizabeth Ritchie Papers
Richard Rodda Papers
Hester Roe Rogers Papers
John Wesley's Will, Olin Library, Wesleyan University, Middletown, Conn.
Zechariah Yewdall Papers

Printed Materials

Abelove, Henry. "Jonathan Edwards's Letter of Invitation to George Whitefield," *William and Mary Quarterly*, 24 (July 1972): 487–89.

————. "John Wesley's Influence During His Lifetime on the Methodists." Ph.D. dissertation, Yale University, 1978.

————. "Some Speculations on the History of 'Sexual Intercourse' During the 'Long Eighteenth Century' in England," *Genders*, 6 (Nov. 1989): 125–30.

Agnew, Jean-Christophe. *Worlds Apart*. Cambridge, Eng., 1986.

Andrews, Edward Deming. *The People Called Shakers: A Search for a Perfect Society*. Oxford, 1953.

Anstey, Christopher. *New Bath Guide*. 4th ed. London, 1767.

Arnold, Janet. *Perukes and Periwigs*. London, 1970.

Atmore, Charles. *The Methodist Memorial; Being an Impartial Sketch of the Lives and Characters of the Preachers, Who Have Departed This Life Since the Commencement of the Work of God Among the People Called Methodists, Late in Connection with the Rev. John Wesley, Deceased*. Bristol, 1801.

Autobiography of Francis Place, ed. Mary Thrale. Cambridge, Eng., 1972.

Baker, Frank. *Charles Wesley as Revealed by His Letters*. Wesley Historical Society Lecture no. 14. London, 1948.

————. *John Wesley and the Church of England*. Nashville, Tenn., 1970.

————. "John Wesley's First Marriage," *London Quarterly and Holborn Review*, 192 (Oct. 1967): 305–15.

————. "Methodism and Literature in the Eighteenth Century," *Proceedings of the Wesley Historical Society*, 22 (Sept. 1946): 1181–83.

————. "The People Called Methodists—3. Polity," in Rupert Davies and Gordon Rupp, eds., *A History of the Methodist Church in Great Britain*, vol. 1, pp. 211–55. London, 1965.

————. *A Union Catalogue of the Publications of John and Charles Wesley*. Durham, N.C., 1966

Barish, Jonas. "Exhibitionism and the Anti-theatrical Prejudice," *ELH: A Journal of English Literary History*, 36 (March 1969): 1–29.

Beaumont, Joseph. *Memoirs of Mrs. Mary Tatham, Late of Nottingham*. New York, 1839.

Bennet, William. *Memoirs of Mrs. Grace Bennet*. Macclesfield, Eng., 1803.

The Bishop of Exeter's Answer to Mr. J. Wesley's Late Letter to His Lordship. London, 1752.

Black, Eugene. *The Association: British Extraparliamentary Organization, 1769–1793*. Cambridge, Mass., 1963.

Bradburn, Eliza Weaver. *Memoirs of the Late Rev. Samuel Bradburn; Con-*

sisting Principally of a Narrative of His Early Life, Written by Himself; and Extracts from a Journal to Which Is Added a Selection from His Manuscripts. London, 1816.

Brantley, Richard E. *Wordsworth's Natural Methodism*. New Haven, Conn., 1975.

Bretherton, Francis. *Early Methodism in and around Chester, 1749–1812*. Chester, 1903.

Brewer, John. *Party Ideology and Popular Politics at the Accession of George III*. Cambridge, Eng., 1976.

Brockbank, W., and F. Kenworthy, eds., *Diary of Richard Kay, 1716–51, of Baldingstone near Bury*, Chetham Society, 3d series, vol. 16. Manchester, 1968.

Brooke, Susan. "Journal of Isabella MacKiver," *Proceedings of the Wesley Historical Society*, 28 (March 1952): 159–63.

Brown, Peter. *The Body and Society: Men, Women, and Sexual Renunciation in Early Christianity*. New York, 1988.

Buck, Anne. *Dress in Eighteenth-Century England*. New York, 1979.

Bunting, Thomas Percival. *Life of Jabez Bunting, D.D.*, vol. 1. London, 1859.

Burdsall, Richard. *Memoirs of the Life of Richard Burdsall*. 3d ed. Thetford, 1823.

Bushman, Richard, ed. *The Great Awakening*. Williamsburg, Va., 1970.

Butler, Jon. "Enthusiasm Described and Decried: The Great Awakening as Interpretative Fiction," *Journal of American History*, 69 (1982): 305–25.

Caldwell, Patricia. *The Puritan Conversion Narrative*. Cambridge, Eng., 1983.

Chalmers, A., ed. *The British Essayists*. "The Connoisseur," vols. 24, 25. London, 1823.

Christie, O. F., ed. *Diary of the Rev'd William Jones, 1777–1821*. London, 1929.

Church, Leslie. *The Early Methodist People*. London, 1948.

———. *More About the Early Methodist People*. London, 1949.

Cook, F. S. *Walcott Methodist Church and Early Methodism in Bath*. Bath, n.d.

Coupe, S. L., James Howarth, and Hugh Taylor. *Wesleyan Methodism in Bagslate*. Bagslate, 1910.

Cozzens-Hardy, Basil, ed. *Diary of Sylas Neville*. Oxford, 1950.

Curnock, Nehemiah, ed. *The Journal of the Rev. John Wesley, A.M.*, 8 vols. London, 1909–16.

Currie, Robert. "A Micro-Theory of Methodist Growth," *Proceedings of the Wesley Historical Society*, 36 (Oct. 1967): 65–73.

Currie, Robert, Alan Gilbert, and Lee Horsley. *Churches and Churchgoers: Patterns of Church Growth in the British Isles Since 1700.* Oxford, Eng., 1977.

Davidson, James West. *The Logic of Millennial Thought: Eighteenth-Century New England.* New Haven, Conn., 1977.

Davies, Horton. *Worship and Theology in England, 1690–1850.* Princeton, N.J., 1961.

Davis, David Brion. *The Problem of Slavery in Western Culture.* Ithaca, N.Y., 1966.

Dickinson, Robert. *Life of the Rev. John Braithwaite.* London, 1825.

Dobson, William, ed. *Extracts from the Diary of the Rev. Peter Walkden, Non-Conformist Minister, for the Years 1725, 1729, and 1730.* Preston, 1866.

Dolbey, George. *Architectural Expression of Methodism: The First Hundred Years.* London, 1964.

Dreyer, Frederick. "Faith and Experience in the Thought of John Wesley," *American Historical Review,* 88 (Feb. 1983): 12–30.

Driver, Cecil. *Tory Radical: The Life of Richard Oastler.* Oxford, 1946.

Dunn, Samuel. *Memoirs of Mr. Tho. Tatham and of Wesley on Methodism in Nottingham.* London, 1847.

Dyson, J. B. *History of Wesleyan Methodism in the Congleton Circuit.* London, 1856.

Efficacy of Faith in the Atonement of Christ: Exemplified in a Memoir of Mr. William Carvasso, Written by Himself and Edited by His Son. 11th ed. London, 1847.

Everett, James. *Adam Clarke Portrayed.* 3 vols. London, 1843.

Everitt, Alan. *The Pattern of Rural Dissent: The Nineteenth Century.* Department of English Local History, Occasional Papers, 2d series, no. 4. Leicester, 1972.

Extracts from the Leeds Mercury, *1737–1742.* Thoresby Society, vol. 26. Leeds, 1919–22.

Foucault, Michel. *The History of Sexuality.* Vol. 1, *An Introduction* (New York, 1980); vol. 2, *The Use of Pleasure* (New York, 1985); vol. 3, *The Care of the Self* (New York, 1986).

Freud, Sigmund. "The Dynamics of Transference," in vol. 12 of James Strachey et al., eds., *Standard Edition of the Complete Psychological Writings of Sigmund Freud,* 24 vols. London, 1954–66, pp. 97–108.

———. *Group Psychology and the Analysis of the Ego,* in vol. 18 of James Strachey et al., eds., *Standard Edition of the Complete Psychological Writings of Sigmund Freud.* London, 1954–66, pp. 67–143.

"A Friend of Wesley," *Proceedings of the Wesley Historical Society,* 22 (March 1940): 117–18.

Gardiner, Samuel R. *History of England from the Accession of James I to the Outbreak of the Civil War*, vol. 1. London, 1884.

Gaustad, Edwin Scott. *The Great Awakening in New England*. New York, 1957.

Gazetteer and New Daily Advertiser, 1775.

Gentleman's Magazine, 1740–91.

Gilbert, Alan D. *Religion and Society in Industrial England*. London, 1976.

Gilboy, Elizabeth W. *Wages in Eighteenth Century England*. Harvard Economic Studies, vol. 45. Cambridge, Mass., 1934.

Gill, Frederick. *In the Steps of John Wesley*. London, 1962.

Gillies, John, ed. *Historical Collections Relating to the Remarkable Success of the Gospel, and Eminent Instruments Employed in Promoting It*. 2 vols. Glasgow, 1754.

Gilsdorf, Joy. "The Puritan Apocalypse." Ph.D. dissertation, Yale University, 1964.

Goen, C. C. *Revivalism and Separatism in New England*. New Haven, Conn., 1962.

Gollin, Gillian. *Moravians in Two Worlds: A Study of Changing Communities*. New York, 1967.

Goss, W. A. "Early Methodism in Bristol," *Proceedings of the Wesley Historical Society*, 19 (Sept. 1934): 161–68.

Green, Richard. *Anti-Methodist Publications Issued During the Eighteenth Century*. London, 1902.

Green, V. H. H. *John Wesley*. London, 1964.

Habakkuk, H. J. "England," in A. Goodwin, ed., *The European Nobility in the Eighteenth Century*. Rev. ed. New York, 1967, 1–21.

Halévy, Élie. *The Birth of Methodism in England*, tr. Bernard Semmel. Chicago, 1971.

Hall, David D. *The Faithful Shepherd*. Chapel Hill, N.C., 1972.

Haller, William. *The Rise of Puritanism*. New York, 1938.

Haller, William, and Malleville. "The Puritan Art of Love," *Huntington Library Quarterly*, 5 (Jan. 1942): 235–72.

Hartshorne, Albert, ed. *Memoirs of a Royal Chaplain, 1729–1763: The Correspondence of Edmund Pyle, D.D., Chaplain in Ordinary to George II with Samuel Kerrick, D.D., Vicar of Dersingham, Rector of Wolferton, and Rector of Western Norton*. London, 1905.

Herbert, Thomas. *John Wesley as Editor and Author*. Princeton Studies in English. Princeton, N.J., 1940.

Heyrman, Christine. *Commerce and Culture: The Maritime Communities of Colonial Massachusetts, 1690–1750*. New York, 1984.

Hill, A. Wesley. *John Wesley Among the Physicians: A Study of Eighteenth Century Medicine.* Wesley Historical Society Lecture no. 24. London, 1958.

Hill, Christopher. *The World Turned Upside Down.* New York, 1972.

Hilliard, David. "UnEnglish and Unmanly: Anglo-Catholicism and Homosexuality," *Victorian Studies,* 25 (Winter 1982), 181–210.

Hirschberg, D. "A Social History of the Anglican Episcopate, 1660–1760." Ph.D. dissertation, University of Michigan, 1976.

The Homes, Haunts, and Friends of John Wesley: Being the Centenary Number of the Methodist Recorder. Rev. and enlarged ed. London, 1891.

Hoole, Elijah. "Dr. Kennicott and Mr. Wesley's Last Sermon at St. Mary's, Oxford," *Wesleyan Methodist Magazine,* 5th series, 12 (Jan. 1866), 47.

Jackson, Thomas, ed. *The Lives of the Early Methodist Preachers, Chiefly Written by Themselves.* 3 vols. London, 1838.

Janion, J. *Some Account of the Introducton of Methodism into the City, and Some Parts, of the County, of Chester.* Chester, 1833.

Jemison, Margaret, ed. *A Methodist Courtship: Love Letters of Joseph Benson and Sarah Thompson, 1779–1780.* Atlanta, Ga., 1945.

Jordanova, Ludmilla. "The Popularization of Medicine: Tissot on Onanism," *Textual Practice,* 1 (1987): 68–80.

Judge, G. H. B. "Methodism in Whitehaven," *Proceedings of the Wesley Historical Society,* 19 (March 1933): 25–29.

———. *Origins and Progress of Wesleyan Methodism in Cheltenham and District.* Cheltenham, 1912.

King, Lester. *The Medical World of the Eighteenth Century.* Chicago, 1958.

Lacan, Jacques. *The Four Fundamental Concepts of Psychoanalysis.* New York, 1978.

Lackington, James. *Memoirs of James Lackington, Written by Himself.* New York, 1796.

Laqueur, Thomas. *Religion and Respectability.* New Haven, Conn., 1976.

Lecky, William Hartpole. *A History of England in the Eighteenth Century,* vol. 2. London, 1883.

Lee, Philip. "Thomas Maxfield," *Proceedings of the Wesley Historical Society,* 21 (Sept. 1938): 161–63.

Leger, J. A. *John Wesley's Last Love.* London, 1910.

Life of Henry Longden, Minister of the Gospel, Compiled from His Memoirs, Diary, Letters, and Other Authentic Documents. New York, 1837.

Lindström, Harald. *Wesley and Sanctification.* Stockholm, 1946.

Linnell, C. S., ed. *Diaries of Thomas Wilson, D.D.* London, 1964.

London Chronicle, 1775.

London Packet, 1775.

Lovejoy, David S. *Religious Enthusiasm in the New World.* Cambridge, Mass., 1985.

Lowell, Robert. *For the Union Dead.* New York, 1965.

Lyles, Albert. *Methodism Mocked.* London, 1960.

MacDonald, James. *Memoirs of the Rev. Joseph Benson.* London, 1822.

MacDonald, Michael. "Religion, Social Change, and Psychological Healing in England, 1600–1800," in vol. 19 of W. J. Shiels, *The Church and Healing.* Studies in Church History. Oxford, 1982, pp. 101–25.

Macinnes, John. *The Evangelical Movement in the Highlands of Scotland, 1688–1800.* Aberdeen, 1951.

Malcolmson, Robert. *Popular Recreations in English Society, 1700–1850.* Cambridge, Eng., 1973.

Malmgreen, Gail. "Domestic Discords: Women and the Family in East Cheshire Methodism, 1750–1830," in Jim Obelkevich, Lyndal Roper, and Raphael Samuel, eds., *Disciplines of Faith.* London, 1987, pp. 55–70.

Manning, B. L. "Some Characteristics of the Older Dissent," *Congregational Quarterly*, 5 (July 1927), 286–300.

Manning, F. J., ed. *The Williamson Letters.* Publications of the Bedfordshire Historical Record Society, vol. 34. London, 1954.

McKendrick, Neil, John Brewer, and J. H. Plumb, eds. *The Birth of Consumer Society: The Commercialization of Eighteenth Century England.* London, 1983.

McLachlan, Herbert. *Essays and Addresses.* Manchester, 1950.

McLoughlin, William G. *Revivals, Awakenings, and Reform.* Chicago, 1978.

Miller, Perry. *Jonathan Edwards.* New York, 1949.

Minutes of the Methodist Conferences, vol. 1. London, 1862.

Monk, Robert. *John Wesley: His Puritan Heritage.* Nashville, Tenn., 1966.

Morgan, Edmund S., Jr. "The Puritans and Sex," *New England Quarterly*, 15 (Dec. 1942): 591–607.

———. *Visible Saints: The History of a Puritan Idea.* New York, 1963.

Moore, Henry. *The Life of the Rev. John Wesley, A.M.* 2 vols. New York, 1824–26.

Namier, Sir Lewis, and John Brooke. *The House of Commons, 1754–1790.* 3 vols. London, 1964.

Nelson, John. *The Journal of Mr. John Nelson, Preacher of the Gospel, Containing an Account of God's Dealings with Him, From His Youth to the Forty-Second Year of His Age.* London, 1846.

Newton, John A. *Methodism and the Puritans.* Friends of Dr. Williams' Library, lecture no. 18. London, 1964.

Notestein, Wallace. *The House of Commons, 1604–1610.* New Haven, Conn., 1971.

Nuttall, G. *The Holy Spirit in Puritan Faith and Experience.* Oxford, 1946.

Obelkevich, James. *Religion and Rural Society: South Lindsey, 1825–1875.* Oxford, 1976.

O'Brien, Susan. "A Transatlantic Community of Saints: The Great Awakening and the First Evangelical Network, 1735–1755," *American Historical Review*, 91 (Oct. 1986): 811–32.

Original Letters Between the Reverend John Wesley, and Mr. Richard Tompson, Respecting the Doctrine of Assurance, as Held by the Former, Wherein that Tenet is Fully Examined. London, 1760.

Outler, Albert, ed. *John Wesley.* Library of Christian Thought. New York, 1964.

Ozment, Steven. "Marriage and Ministry in the Protestant Churches," in William Bassett and Peter Huizing, eds., *Celibacy in the Church*, pp. 39–56. New York, 1972.

Paragraph, Peter. *The Methodist and Mimick: A Tale in Hudibrastic Verse.* 2d ed. London, 1767.

Pawlyn, John L. *Bristol Methodism in John Wesley's Day.* Bristol, 1877.

Popkin, Richard, H., ed. *Millenarianism and Messianism in English Literature and Thought, 1650–1800.* Leiden, 1988.

Porter, Roy. "Medicine and the Enlightenment in Eighteenth-Century England," *Society for the Social History of Medicine Bulletin*, 25 (1979), 27–41.

———. *Mind Forg'd Manacles: A History of Madness in England from the Restoration to the Regency.* Cambridge, Mass., 1987.

Riggall, M. "Hairdressers' Charges in Wesley's Time," *Proceedings of the Wesley Historical Society*, 13 (June 1922): 142–43.

Riley, Edward Miles, ed. *The Journal of John Harrower: An Indentured Servant in the Colony of Virginia, 1773–1776.* Williamsburg, Va., 1963.

Rogers, James. *The Experience and Labours of James Rogers, Preacher of the Gospel.* Bristol, 1796.

Rousseau, George S. "John Wesley's Primitive Physick, 1747," *Harvard Library Bulletin*, 16 (1968): 242–56.

———. "The Pursuit of Homosexuality in the Eighteenth Century: Utterly Confused Category and/or Rich Repository?," in Robert Parks Maccubin, ed., *'Tis Nature's Fault: Unauthorized Sexuality During the Enlightenment.* Cambridge, Eng., 1987, pp. 132–68.

Rowe, G. Stringer. "John Wesley's Wig," *Proceedings of the Wesley Historical Society*, 6 (June 1907): 27–28.

Sachse, Julius Friedrich. *The German Sectarians of Pennsylvania, 1708–1742:*

A Critical and Legendary History of the Ephrata Cloister and the Dunkers. 2 vols. Philadelphia, 1899–1900.

Schwartz, Hillel. *The French Prophets: The History of a Millenarian Group in Eighteenth-Century England*. Berkeley, Calif., 1980.

Sedgwick, Romney, ed. *The House of Commons, 1715–1754*. 2 vols. London, 1970.

A Select Collection of the Letters of the Late George Whitefield. 3 vols. London, 1772.

Semmel, Bernard. *The Methodist Revolution*. New York, 1973.

Shaw, Thomas. *A History of Cornish Methodism*. Truro, 1967.

Shepherd, T. B. *Methodism and the Literature of the Eighteenth Century*. London, 1940.

A Short Account of the Experiences of Mrs. Hester Ann Rogers. New York, 1811.

Smollett, Tobias. *The Expedition of Humphrey Clinker*, ed. H. M. Jones. London, 1943.

Some Papers Giving An Account of the Rise and Progress of Methodism at Wednesbury in Staffordshire and other Parishes Adjacent: As likewise of the late Riot in those Parts. London, 1744.

Steele, Anthony. *History of Methodism in Barnard Castle*. London, 1857.

Stengers, Jean, and Anne Van Neck. *Histoire d'une grande peur: la masturbation*. Brussels, 1984.

Stevenson, George J. *City Road Chapel, London, and Its Associations*. London, n.d.

———. *Memorials of the Wesley Family*. New York, 1876.

Stokes, Francis Griffin, ed. *Blecheley Diary of the Rev. William Cole, 1765–1767*. London, 1913.

Stone, Lawrence. *The Family, Sex, and Marriage in England, 1500–1800*. New York, 1977.

Strachan, Alexander. *Recollections of the Life and Times of the late Rev. George Lowe*. London, 1848.

Summerson, John. *Georgian London*. Rev. ed. London, 1962.

Telford, John. *Wesley's Chapel and Wesley's House*. Rev. ed. London, 1926.

———, ed. *The Letters of the Rev. John Wesley, A.M.* 8 vols. London, 1931.

Thompson, E. P. *The Making of the English Working Class*. Rev. ed. London, 1968.

———. "Patrician Society, Plebeian Culture," *Journal of Social History*, 7 (Summer 1974), pp. 382–405.

Tissot, Samuel. *Onanism; or a Treatise Upon the Disorders Produced by Masturbation*, tr. A. Hume. London, 1766.

Told, Silas. *An Account of the Life and Dealings of God with Silas Told, Late*

Preacher of the Gospel, Wherein Is Set Forth the Wonderful Display of Divine Providence towards Him when at Sea; His Various Sufferings Abroad; Together with Many Instances of the Sovereign Grace of God, in the Conversion of Several Malefactors under Sentence of Death, Who Were Greatly Blessed under His Ministry. London, 1786.

Town and Country Magazine, or Universal Repository of Knowledge, Instruction, and Entertainment. Supplement to the Year 1774.

Townsend, James. *History of Darwen Wesleyan Methodism.* Rossendale and Stockport, 1916.

Townsend, W. J., H. B. Workman, and George Eayrs, eds., *A New History of Methodism,* vol. 1. London, 1909.

Treffrey, Richard. *Memoirs of Mr. Richard Trewavas, Sr., of Mousehole Cornwall: to Which is Prefixed an Account of Methodism in Mousehole.* London, 1839.

Trumbach, Randolph. "London's Sodomites: Homosexual Behavior and Western Culture in the Eighteenth Century," *Journal of Social History,* 11 (1977): 11–22.

———. *The Rise of the Egalitarian Family.* New York, 1978.

"The Twelve Rules of a Helper," *Proceedings of the Wesley Historical Society,* 7 (Dec. 1909): 82–83.

Tyerman, Luke. *The Life and Times of the Rev. John Wesley, A.M.* 2d ed., 3 vols. London, 1870–72.

———. *Wesley's Designated Successor.* New York, 1883.

Valenze, Deborah. *Prophetic Sons and Daughters.* Princeton, N.J., 1985.

Vendler, Helen. *The Poetry of George Herbert.* Cambridge, Mass., 1975.

Walsh, John. "Methodism and the Mob in the Eighteenth Century," in G. J. Cuming and Derek Baker, eds., *Popular Belief and Practice.* Studies in Church History, no. 8. Cambridge, Eng., 1972, pp. 213–27.

———. "Methodism at the End of the Eighteenth Century," in Rupert Davies and Gordon Rupp, eds., *A History of the Methodist Church in Great Britain,* vol. 1. London 1965, pp. 275–315.

[A letter, number, or other designation in brackets following the entry indicates the printing or edition used in Frank Baker, *Union Catalogue of the Publications of John and Charles Wesley.*]

Wesley, John. *The Desideratum; Or Electricity Made Plain and Useful.* 3d ed. London, 1790. [3]

———. *Free Grace: A Sermon Preach'd at Bristol.* 4th ed. London, 1754. [4]

———. *God's Love to Fallen Man: A Sermon on Romans V. 15.* London, 1791.

———. *The Nature, Design, and General Rules of the United Societies in*

London, Bristol, Kingswood, and Newcastle-upon-Tyne. 4th ed. London, 1744. [4]

——. *A Plain Account of Christian Perfection.* London, 1820. [12]

——. *Primitive Physick: or, An Easy and Natural Method of Curing Most Diseases.* 15th ed., corrected and much enlarged. London, 1772. [15]

——. *The Protestant Association: Written in the Midst of the Tumults.* London, 1781. [Probably by John or Charles Wesley.]

——. *Queries Proposed to the Right Reverend and Right Honourable Count Zinzendorf.* London, 1755. [first listing]

——. *Remember the Sabbath Day.* N.p., n.d. [G]

——. *A Short Account of the School in Kingswood near Bristol.* Bristol, 1749. [first listing]

——. *Swear Not at All.* N.p., n.d. [A]

——. *Thoughts on Marriage and a Single Life.* Bristol, 1743. [1b]

——. *Thoughts on the Sin of Onan, Chiefly Extracted from a Late Writer.* London, 1767. [first listing]

——. *Thoughts on a Single Life.* London, 1765. [first listing]

Westerkamp, Marilyn. *Triumph of the Laity: Scots-Irish Piety and the Great Awakening, 1625–1760.* New York, 1988.

White, James. *Protestant Worship and Church Architecture.* Oxford, 1964.

Whitehead, John. *The Life of the Rev. John Wesley, A.M., Sometime Fellow of Lincoln College, Oxford, Collected from His Private Papers and Printed Works; and Written at the Request of His Executors; to which is Prefixed Some Account of His Ancestor and Relations: with the Life of Rev. Charles Wesley, M.A., Collected from His Private Journal, and Never Before Published; the Whole Forming a History of Methodism, in which the Principles and Economy of the Methodists are Unfolded.* 2 vols. London, 1796.

Whiting, C. E., ed. *Two Yorkshire Diaries.* Yorkshire Archaeological Society Record Series vol. 117. Leeds, 1952.

Wrigley, E. A. "Family Limitation in Pre-Industrial England," in Orest and Patricia Ranum, eds., *Popular Attitudes Toward Birth Control in Pre-Industrial England.* New York, 1972, pp. 53–99.

Wrigley, E. A., and R. S. Schofield. *The Population History of England: A Reconstruction.* London, 1981.

INDEX

Index

Library of Congress Cataloging-in-Publication Data

Abelove, Henry.

   The evangelist of desire : John Wesley and the Methodists / Henry
Abelove.

        p.   cm.

   Includes bibliographical references.

   Includes index.

   ISBN 0-8047-1826-1 (alk. paper)

      1. Wesley, John, 1703–1791—Influence.   2. Wesley, John,
1703–1791—Disciples.   3. Methodists—England—History—18th
century.   I. Title.

BX8495.W5A64

287′.092—dc20

[B]   90-35420

                                                                                 CIP

   ♾ This book is printed on acid-free paper.